THE NATION'S
FAVOURITE
POEMS OF CHILDHOOD

The 10 most popular poems from the *Radio Times* poll
to find the nation's favourite childhood poem.

1. I Remember, I Remember
THOMAS HOOD

2. The Land of Counterpane
ROBERT LOUIS STEVENSON

3. Timothy Winters
CHARLES CAUSLEY

4. The Toys
COVENTRY PATMORE

5. Matilda
HILAIRE BELLOC

6. The Lamplighter
ROBERT LOUIS STEVENSON

7. Hiawatha's Childhood
H. W. LONGFELLOW

8. Fern Hill
DYLAN THOMAS

9. The Children's Hour
H. W. LONGFELLOW

10. Walking Away
C. DAY LEWIS

*

THE NATION'S FAVOURITE POEMS OF CHILDHOOD

— ◇ —

FOREWORD BY
ESTHER RANTZEN OBE

Published by
BBC Worldwide Limited,
Woodlands,
80 Wood Lane,
London
W12 0TT

First published 2000
Edited and compiled by Alex Warwick
Compilation © BBC Worldwide 2000
Poems © individual copyright holders

ISBN: 0 563 55184 4

Set in Stempel Garamond by Keystroke,
Jacaranda Lodge, Wolverhampton.
Printed and bound in Great Britain by Martins the Printers Ltd,
Berwick-upon-Tweed.
Cover printed by Belmont Press, Northampton.

CONTENTS

— ◇ —

*'My babe so beautiful! it thrills my heart
With tender gladness, thus to look at thee'*

*'A school is where they grind the grain of thought,
And grind the children who must mind the thought'*

– Contents –

'This is the kind of thing I do
when I'm needing attention'

'When my silent terror cried,
Nobody, nobody replied'

– Contents –

– Contents –

'... The glamour
Of childish days is upon me, my manhood is cast
Down in the flood of remembrance, I weep
like a child for the past'

'It is not now as it hath been of yore –
Turn whereso'er I may, . . .
The things which I have seen I now can
see no more'

– Contents –

FOREWORD BY ESTHER RANTZEN OBE

— ◇ —

All children love poetry. From the moment we hear 'the cat sat on the mat' and 'Sing a Song of Sixpence', poems become the way we learn and celebrate, the stuff of jokes, the happy birthday song. My sister and I used to chant reams of verse from A. A. Milne and Robert Louis Stevenson. My godmother read them to us in our country garden, and I remember the tragic moment when the book shut at bedtime. I can still recite chunks of Lewis Carroll's 'The Walrus and the Carpenter', learned at my grandmother's knee. There was a magic about the way the words fell, the heartbeat of a regular metre, the satisfaction when a rhyme was a perfect fit. No wonder that so many poets love children, when the very young are such an enthusiastic audience.

This is not a book of poems for children, however. These are poems about particular moments of childhood remembered or observed. It is not a sentimental collection. No anthology that includes Hilaire Belloc and Philip Larkin could be accused of that. But every other aspect of childhood is here, the humour, the enthusiasm, the mystery, the frustration. If you have forgotten the joy of a toddler holding your hand, read Stephen Spender's poem 'To My Daughter' to remind yourself, written as he walks with his daughter, the 'Bright clasp of her whole hand around my finger'. It is not all nostalgia bathed in sunshine, however, Howard Nemerov recreates the foreboding of his son's first day at school, 'A school is where they grind the grain of thought,' he says, 'And grind the children who must mind the thought'. Fleur Adcock takes on the adolescent rebellion in 'For Heidi with Blue Hair', a deceptively witty poem with a serious twist. There are poems by Betjeman, and McGough, and beside them the visionaries such as Blake and Wordsworth.

If you hate children, you won't enjoy this book, but then if you hate children, you'll doubtless hate poetry, too. For the rest of us, what this enchanting books reveals is that poets and children have a great deal in common; imagination, unpredictability, and a delight in words.

'My babe so beautiful! it thrills my heart
With tender gladness, thus to look at thee'

from 'Frost at Midnight'

THOMAS BASTARD 1566–1618

DE PUERO BALBUTIENTE

Methinks 'tis pretty sport to hear a child
Rocking a word in mouth yet undefiled;
The tender racquet rudely plays the sound
Which, weakly bandied, cannot back rebound;
And the soft air the softer roof doth kiss
With a sweet dying and a pretty miss,
Which hears no answer yet from the white rank
Of teeth not risen from their coral bank.
The alphabet is searched for letters soft
To try a word before it can be wrought;
And when it slideth forth, it goes as nice
As when a man doth walk upon the ice.

AMBROSE PHILIPS 1674–1749

TO MISS CHARLOTTE PULTENEY IN HER MOTHER'S ARMS

Timely blossom, infant fair,
Fondling of a happy pair,
Every morn and every night,
Their solicitous delight,
Sleeping, waking, still at ease,
Pleasing, without skill to please,
Little gossip, blithe and hale,
Tattling many a broken tale,
Singing many a tuneless song,
Lavish of a heedless tongue,
Simple maiden, void of art,
Babbling out the very heart,
Yet abandoned to thy will,
Yet imagining no ill,
Yet too innocent to blush,
Like the linlet in the bush,
To the mother-linnet's note
Moduling her slender throat,
Chirping forth thy petty joys,
Wanton in the change of toys,
Like the linnet green in May,
Flitting to each bloomy spray,
Wearied then, and glad of rest,
Like the linlet in the nest.
This thy present happy lot,
This, in time, will be forgot:
Other pleasures, other cares,
Ever-busy time prepares;
And thou shalt in thy daughter see
This picture, once, resembled thee.

ROBERT BURNS 1759–96

_____

A POET'S WELCOME TO HIS LOVE-BEGOTTEN DAUGHTER; THE FIRST INSTANCE THAT ENTITLED HIM TO THE VENERABLE APPELLATION OF FATHER

Thou's welcome, wean! Mischanter fa' me,
If thoughts o' thee, or yet thy Mamie,
Shall ever daunton me or awe me,
My bonie lady;
Or if I blush when thou shalt ca' me
Tyta, or Daddie.

Though now they ca' me fornicator,
And tease my name in kintra clatter,
The mair they talk, I'm kend the better;
E'en let them clash!
An auld wife's tongue's a feckless matter
To gie ane fash.

Welcome! My bonie, sweet, wee dochter!
Though ye come here a wee unsought for;
And though your comin I hae fought for,
Baith Kirk and Queir;
Yet by my faith, ye're no unwrought for,
That I shall swear!

Wee image o' my bonie Betty,
As fatherly I kiss and daut thee,
As dear and near my heart I set thee,
Wi' as gude will,
As a' the Priests had seen me get thee
That's out o' h—.

Sweet fruit o' monie a merry dint,
My funny toil is no a' tint;
Though ye come to the warld asklent,
Which fools may scoff at,
In my last plack your part's be in't,
The better half o't.

Though I should be the waur bestead,
Thou's be as braw and bienly clad,
And thy young years as nicely bred
              Wi' education,
As any brat o' Wedlock's bed,
              In a' thy station.

Lord grant that thou may ay inherit
Thy Mither's looks an' gracefu' merit;
An' thy poor, worthless Daddie's spirit,
              Without his failins!
'Twad please me mair to see thee heir it
              Than stocked mailins!

For if thou be, what I wad hae thee,
And tak the counsel I shall gie thee,
I'll never rue my trouble wi' thee,
              The cost nor shame o't,
But be a loving Father to thee,
              And brag the name o't.

JOANNA BAILLIE 1762–1851

A MOTHER TO HER WAKING INFANT

Now in thy dazzling half-oped eye,
Thy curlèd nose and lip awry,
Thy up-hoist arms and noddling head,
And little chin with crystal spread,
Poor helpless thing! what do I see,
   That I should sing of thee?

From thy poor tongue no accents come,
Which can but rub thy toothless gum;
Small understanding boasts thy face.
Thy shapeless limbs nor step nor grace;
A few short words thy feats may tell.
   And yet I love thee well.

When sudden wakes the bitter shriek,
And redder swells thy little cheek;
When rattled keys thy woes beguile,
And through the wet eye gleams the smile,
Still for thy weakly self is spent
   Thy little silly plaint.

But when thy friends are in distress,
Thou'lt laugh and chuckle ne'er the less;
Nor e'en with sympathy be smitten,
Though all are sad but thee and kitten;
Yet little varlet that thou art,
   Thou twitchest at the heart.

Thy rosy cheek so soft and warm;
Thy pinky hand and dimpled arm;
Thy silken locks that scantly peep,
With gold-tipped ends, where circles deep
Around thy neck in harmless grace
So soft and sleekly hold their place,
Might harder hearts with kindness fill,
   And gain our right good will.

Each passing clown bestows his blessing,
Thy mouth is worn with old wives' kissing:
E'en lighter looks the gloomy eye
Of surly sense, when thou art by;
And yet I think whoe'er they be,
    They love thee not like me.

Perhaps when time shall add a few
Short years to thee, thou'lt love me too.
Then wilt thou through life's weary way
Become my sure and cheering stay:
Wilt care for me, and be my hold,
    When I am weak and old.

Thou'lt listen to my lengthened tale,
And pity me when I am frail —
But see, the sweepy spinning fly
Upon the window takes thine eye,
Go to thy little senseless play —
    Thou dost not heed my lay.

SAMUEL TAYLOR COLERIDGE 1772–1834

FROST AT MIDNIGHT

The Frost performs its secret ministry,
Unhelped by any wind. The owlet's cry
Came loud – and hark, again! loud as before.
The inmates of my cottage, all at rest,
Have left me to that solitude, which suits
Abstruser musings: save that at my side
My cradled infant slumbers peacefully.
'Tis calm indeed! so calm, that it disturbs
And vexes meditation with its strange
And extreme silentness. Sea, hill, and wood,
This populous village! Sea, and hill, and wood,
With all the numberless goings-on of life.
Inaudible as dreams! the thin blue flame
Lies on my low-burnt fire, and quivers not;
Only that film, which fluttered on the grate,
Still flutters there, the sole unquiet thing.
Methinks its motion in this hush of nature
Gives it dim sympathies with me who live,
Making it a companionable form,
Whose puny flaps and freaks the idling Spirit
By its own moods interprets, everywhere
Echo or mirror seeking of itself.
And makes a toy of Thought.

              But O! how oft,
How oft, at school, with most believing mind,
Presageful, have I gazed upon the bars,
To watch that fluttering *stranger!* and as oft
With unclosed lids, already had I dreamt
Of my sweet birthplace, and the old church tower,
Whose bells, the poor man's only music, rang
From morn to evening, all the hot Fair-day,
So sweetly, that they stirred and haunted me
With a wild pleasure, falling on mine ear

Most like articulate sounds of things to come!
So gazed I, till the soothing things, I dreamt,
Lulled me to sleep, and sleep prolonged my dreams!
And so I brooded all the following morn,
Awed by the stern preceptor's face, mine eye
Fixed with mock study on my swimming book:
Save if the door half opened, and I snatched
A hasty glance, and still my heart leaped up,
For still I hoped to see the *stranger's* face,
Townsman, or aunt, or sister more beloved,
My playmate when we both were clothed alike!

Dear Babe, that sleepest cradled by my side,
Whose gentle breathings, heard in this deep calm,
Fill up the interspersèd vacancies
And momentary pauses of the thought!
My babe so beautiful! it thrills my heart
With tender gladness, thus to look at thee,
And think that thou shalt learn far other lore,
And in far other scenes! For I was reared
In the great city, pent 'mid cloisters dim,
And saw nought lovely but the sky and stars.
But *thou*, my babe! shalt wander like a breeze
By lakes and sandy shores, beneath the crags
Of ancient mountain, and beneath the clouds,
Which image in their bulk both lakes and shores
And mountain crags: so shalt thou see and hear
The lovely shapes and sounds intelligible
Of that eternal language, which thy God
Utters, who from eternity doth teach
Himself in all, and all things in himself.
Great universal Teacher! he shall mould
Thy spirit, and by giving make it ask.

Therefore all seasons shall be sweet to thee,
Whether the summer clothe the general earth
With greenness, or the redbreast sit and sing
Betwixt the tufts of snow on the bare branch
Of mossy apple tree, while the nigh thatch
Smokes in the sun-thaw; whether the eave-drops fall
Heard only in the trances of the blast,
Or if the secret ministry of frost
Shall hang them up in silent icicles,
Quietly shining to the quiet Moon.

PERCY BYSSHE SHELLEY 1792–1822

TO WILLIAM SHELLEY

I

The billows on the beach are leaping around it,
    The bark is weak and frail,
The sea looks black, and the clouds that bound it
    Darkly strew the gale.
Come with me, thou delightful child,
Come with me, though the wave is wild,
And the winds are loose, we must not stay,
Or the slaves of the law may rend thee away.

II

They have taken thy brother and sister dear,
    They have made them unfit for thee;
They have withered the smile and dried the tear
    Which should have been sacred to me.
To a blighting faith and a cause of crime
They have bound them slaves in youthly prime,
And they will curse my name and thee
Because we fearless are and free.

III

Come thou, belovèd as thou art;
    Another sleepeth still
Near thy sweet mother's anxious heart,
    Which thou with joy shalt fill,
With fairest smiles of wonder thrown
On that which is indeed our own,
And which in distant lands will be
The dearest playmate unto thee.

IV

Fear not the tyrants will rule for ever,
    Or the priests of the evil faith;
They stand on the brink of that raging river,

Whose waves they have tainted with death.
It is fed from the depths of a thousand dells,
Around them it foams and rages and swells;
And their swords and their sceptres I floating see,
Like wrecks on the surge of eternity.

V

Rest, rest, and shriek not, thou gentle child!
    The rocking of the boat thou fearest,
And the cold spray and the clamour wild? –
    There, sit between us two, thou dearest –
Me and thy mother – well we know
The storm at which thou tremblest so,
With all its dark and hungry graves,
Less cruel than the savage slaves
Who hunt us o'er these sheltering waves.

VI

This hour will in thy memory
    Be a dream of days forgotten long.
We soon shall dwell by the azure sea
Of serene and golden Italy,
Or Greece, the Mother of the free;
    And I will teach thine infant tongue
To call upon those heroes old
In their own language, and will mould
Thy growing spirit in the flame
Of Grecian lore, that by such name
A patriot's birthright thou mayst claim!

W. B. YEATS 1865–1939

A PRAYER FOR MY DAUGHTER

Once more the storm is howling, and half hid
Under this cradle-hood and coverlid
My child sleeps on. There is no obstacle
But Gregory's wood and one bare hill
Whereby the haystack- and roof-levelling wind,
Bred on the Atlantic, can be stayed;
And for an hour I have walked and prayed
Because of the great gloom that is in my mind.

I have walked and prayed for this young child an hour
And heard the sea-wind scream upon the tower,
And under the arches of the bridge, and scream
In the elms above the flooded stream;
Imagining in excited reverie
That the future years had come,
Dancing to a frenzied drum,
Out of the murderous innocence of the sea.

May she be granted beauty and yet not
Beauty to make a stranger's eye distraught,
Or hers before a looking-glass, for such,
Being made beautiful overmuch,
Consider beauty a sufficient end,
Lose natural kindness and maybe
The heart-revealing intimacy
That chooses right, and never find a friend.

Helen being chosen found life flat and dull
And later had much trouble from a fool,
While that great Queen, that rose out of the spray,
Being fatherless could have her way
Yet chose a bandy-leggèd smith for man.
It's certain that fine women eat
A crazy salad with their meat
Whereby the Horn of Plenty is undone.

In courtesy I'd have her chiefly learned;
Hearts are not had as a gift but hearts are earned
By those that are not entirely beautiful;
Yet many, that have played the fool
For beauty's very self, has charm made wise,
And many a poor man that has roved,
Loved and thought himself beloved,
From a glad kindness cannot take his eyes.

May she become a flourishing hidden tree
That all her thoughts may like the linnet be,
And have no business but dispensing round
Their magnanimities of sound,
Nor but in merriment begin a chase,
Nor but in merriment a quarrel.
O may she live like some green laurel
Rooted in one dear perpetual place.

My mind, because the minds that I have loved,
The sort of beauty that I have approved,
Prosper but little, has dried up of late,
Yet knows that to be choked with hate
May well be of all evil chances chief.
If there's no hatred in a mind
Assault and battery of the wind
Can never tear the linnet from the leaf.

An intellectual hatred is the worst,
So let her think opinions are accursed.
Have I not seen the loveliest woman born
Out of the mouth of Plenty's horn,
Because of her opinionated mind
Barter that horn and every good
By quiet natures understood
For an old bellows full of angry wind?

Considering that, all hatred driven hence,
The soul recovers radical innocence
And learns at last that it is self-delighting,
Self-appeasing, self-affrighting,
And that its own sweet will is Heaven's will;
She can, though every face should scowl
And every windy quarter howl
Or every bellows burst, be happy still.

And may her bridegroom bring her to a house
Where all's accustomed, ceremonious;
For arrogance and hatred are the wares
Peddled in the thoroughfares.
How but in custom and in ceremony
Are innocence and beauty born?
Ceremony's a name for the rich horn,
And custom for the spreading laurel tree.

PAUL LAURENCE DUNBAR 1872–1906

LITTLE BROWN BABY

Little brown baby wif spa'klin' eyes,
　Come to yo' pappy an' set on his knee.
What you been doin', suh-makin' san' pies?
　Look at dat bib – you's ez du'ty ez me.
Look at dat mouf – dat's merlasses, I bet;
　Come hyeah, Maria, an' wipe off his han's.
Bees gwine to ketch you an' eat you up yit,
　Bein' so sticky and sweet – goodness lan's!

Little brown baby wif spa'klin' eyes,
　Who's pappy's darlin' an' who's pappy's chile?
Who is it all de day nevah once tries
　Fu' to be cross, er once loses dat smile?
Whah did you git dem teef? My, you's a scamp!
　Whah did dat dimple come f'om in yo' chin?
Pappy do' know you – I b'lieves you's a tramp;
　Mammy, dis hyeah's some ol' straggler got in!

Let's th'ow him outen de do' in de san',
　We do' want stragglers a-layin' 'roun' hyeah;
Let's gin him 'way to de big buggah-man;
　I know he's hidin' erroun' hyeah right neah.
Buggah-man, buggah-man, come in de do',
　Hyeah's a bad boy you kin have fu' to eat.
Mammy an' pappy do' want him no mo',
　Swaller him down f'om his haid to his feet!

Dah, now, I t'ought dat you'd hug me up close.
　Go back, ol' buggah, you sha'n't have dis boy.
He ain't no tramp, ner no straggler, of co'se;
　He's pappy's pa'dner an playmate an joy
Come to you pallet now – go to yo res;
　Wisht you could allus know ease an' cleah skies;
Wisht you could stay jes' a chile on my breas' –
　Little brown baby wif spa'klin' eyes!

LOUIS MACNEICE 1907–63

PRAYER BEFORE BIRTH

I am not yet born; O hear me.
Let not the bloodsucking bat or the rat or the stoat or the
    club-footed ghoul come near me.

I am not yet born, console me.
I fear that the human race may with tall walls wall me,
    with strong drugs dope me, with wise lies lure me,
        on black racks rack me, in blood-baths roll me.

I am not yet born; provide me
With water to dandle me, grass to grow for me, trees to talk
    to me, sky to sing to me, birds and a white light
        in the back of my mind to guide me.

I am not yet born; forgive me
For the sins that in me the world shall commit, my words
    when they speak me, my thoughts when they think me,
        my treason engendered by traitors beyond me,
            my life when they murder by means of my
                hands, my death when they live me.

I am not yet born; rehearse me
In the parts I must play and the cues I must take when
    old men lecture me, bureaucrats hector me, mountains
        frown at me, lovers laugh at me, the white
            waves call me to folly and the desert calls
                me to doom and the beggar refuses
                    my gift and my children curse me.

I am not yet born; O hear me,
Let not the man who is beast or who thinks he is God
    come near me.

E. J. SCOVELL 1907–

CHILD WAKING

The child sleeps in the daytime,
With his abandoned, with his jetsam look,
On the bare mattress, across the cot's corner;
Covers and toys thrown out, a routine labour.

Relaxed in sleep and light,
Face upwards, never so clear a prey to eyes;
Like a walled town, surprised out of the air
– All life called in, yet all laid bare

To the enemy above –
He has taken cover in daylight, gone to ground
In his own short length, his body strong in bleached
Blue cotton and his arms outstretched.

Now he opens eyes but not
To see at first; they reflect the light like snow
And I wait in doubt if he sleeps or wakes, till I see
Slight pain of effort at the boundary,

And hear how the trifling wound
Of bewilderment fetches a caverned cry
As he crosses out of sleep – at once to recover
His place and poise, and smile as I lift him over.

But I recall the blue-
White snowfield of his eyes empty of sight
High between dream and day, and think how there
The soul might rise visible as a flower.

STEPHEN SPENDER 1909–95

TO MY DAUGHTER

Bright clasp of her whole hand around my finger
My daughter, as we walk together now.
All my life I'll feel a ring invisibly
Circle this bone with shining: when she is grown
Far from today as her eyes are far already.

R. S. THOMAS 1913–

THE UNBORN DAUGHTER

On her unborn in the vast circle
Concentric with our finite lives;
On her unborn, her name uncurling
Like a young fern within the mind;
On her unclothed with flesh or beauty
In the womb's darkness, I bestow
The formal influence of the will,
The wayward influence of the heart,
Weaving upon her fluid bones
The subtle fabric of her being,
Hair, hands and eyes, the body's texture,
Shot with the glory of the soul.

DYLAN THOMAS 1914–53

from UNDER MILK WOOD

POLLY GARTER
Nothing grows in our garden, only washing. And babies. And where's their fathers live, my love? Over the hills and far away. You're looking up at me now. I know what you're thinking, you poor little milky creature. You're thinking, you're no better than you should be, Polly, and that's good enough for me. Oh, isn't life a terrible thing, thank God?

PHILIP LARKIN 1922–85

_____

BORN YESTERDAY
For Sally Amis

Tightly-folded bud,
I have wished you something
None of the others would:
Not the usual stuff
About being beautiful,
Or running off a spring
Of innocence and love –
They will all wish you that,
And should it prove possible,
Well, you're a lucky girl.

But if it shouldn't, then
May you be ordinary;
Have, like other women,
An average of talents:
Not ugly, not good-looking,
Nothing uncustomary
To pull you off your balance,
That, unworkable itself,
Stops all the rest from working.
In fact, may you be dull –
If that is what a skilled,
Vigilant, flexible,
Unemphasised, enthralled
Catching of happiness is called.

20 January 1954

TED HUGHES 1930–98

FULL MOON AND LITTLE FRIEDA

A cool small evening shrunk to a dog bark and the
    clank of a bucket –

And you listening.
A spider's web, tense for the dew's touch.
A pail lifted, still and brimming – mirror
To tempt a first star to a tremor.

Cows are going home in the lane there, looping the
    hedges with their warm wreaths of breath –
A dark river of blood, many boulders,
Balancing unspilled milk.

'Moon!' you cry suddenly, 'Moon! Moon!'
The moon has stepped back like an artist gazing
    amazed at a work
That points at him amazed.

SYLVIA PLATH 1932–63

MORNING SONG

Love set you going like a fat gold watch.
The midwife slapped your footsoles, and your bald cry
Took its place among the elements.

Our voices echo, magnifying your arrival. New statue.
In a drafty museum, your nakedness
Shadows our safety. We stand round blankly as walls.

I'm no more your mother
Than the cloud that distills a mirror to reflect its own slow
Effacement at the wind's hand.

All night your moth-breath
Flickers among the flat pink roses. I wake to listen:
A far sea moves in my ear.

One cry, and I stumble from bed, cow-heavy and floral
In my Victorian nightgown.
Your mouth opens clean as a cat's. The window square

Whitens and swallows its dull stars. And now you try
Your handful of notes;
The clear vowels rise like balloons.

SYLVIA PLATH 1932–63

YOU'RE

Clownlike, happiest on your hands,
Feet to the stars, and moon-skulled,
Gilled like a fish. A Common-sense
Thumbs-down on the dodo's mode.
Wrapped up in yourself like a spool,
Trawling your dark as owls do.
Mute as a turnip from the Fourth
Of July to All Fool's Day,
O high-riser, my little loaf.

Vague as fog and looked for like mail.
Farther off than Australia.
Bent-backed Atlas, our travelled prawn.
Snug as a bud and at home
Like a sprat in a pickle jug.
A creel of eels, all ripples.
Jumpy as a Mexican bean.
Right, like a well-done sum.
A clean slate, with your own face on.

NIGEL FORDE 1944–

AND SOME OF THE LARGER PIECES THAT YOU SEE ARE CALLED UNCLES
For Fionn

A small, daily miracle; and you
are separate now.

Not separate enough to say
hallo to, but you've come
suddenly. You are.
As if to be were easy.

You lie in a loud tangle of birthdays.
Only one of them
your own.

Beside your cot is the world
we left there on the last night
before you were born. Now
it contains you. Elementary
metaphysics, and easy for
the finger of God, but some of us
like to be surprised by it still.

This is the world, then. It contains,
apart from you and me (and I
am one, according to Shelley,
of its unacknowledged legislators):
calves, that make far woodwind sounds
in brimming meadows; owls
that do the same thing after dark;
lupins, shoelaces, mineral deposits
and the Royal College of Heralds.
A variety of hats, sundials, people
who look a bit like someone else you know,

restored water-mills, presents
from Weston-super-Mare; hippopotamuses,
things with lids, lighthouses, gloves,
Reader's Digest Condensed Books,
things without lids, and one
Great Pyramid of Cheops.

Someone has also invented waves,
silk hayfields, music
and the considerate stars.
We're keeping them for you.

All of a sudden
I'm worried that you're not going
to like them.

There are things you can change.
Already your limbs stammer
as sharp as words. You've made
your first, tiny addendum
to the world's dictionary
as you take fistfuls of air
and squeeze them dry.

'A school is where they grind the grain of thought,
And grind the children who must mind the thought'

from 'September, The First Day of School'

WILLIAM BLAKE 1757–1827

THE SCHOOLBOY

I love to rise in a summer morn
When the birds sing on every tree;
The distant huntsman winds his horn,
And the sky-lark sings with me.
O! what sweet company.

But to go to school in a summer morn,
O! it drives all joy away;
Under a cruel eye outworn,
The little ones spend the day
In sighing and dismay.

Ah! then at times I drooping sit,
And spend many an anxious hour,
Nor in my book can I take delight,
Nor sit in learning's bower,
Worn thro' with the dreary shower.

How can the bird that is born for joy
Sit in a cage and sing?
How can a child, when fears annoy,
But droop his tender wing,
And forget his youthful spring?

O! father & mother, if buds are nip'd
And blossoms blown away,
And if the tender plants are strip'd
Of their joy in the springing day,
By sorrow and care's dismay,

How shall the summer arise in joy,
Or the summer fruits appear?
Or how shall we gather what griefs destroy,
Or bless the mellowing year,
When the blasts of winter appear?

C. DAY LEWIS 1904–72

WALKING AWAY
For Sean

It is eighteen years ago, almost to the day –
A sunny day with the leaves just turning,
The touch-lines new-ruled – since I watched you play
Your first game of football, then, like a satellite
Wrenched from its orbit, go drifting away

Behind a scatter of boys. I can see
You walking away from me towards the school
With the pathos of a half-fledged thing set free
Into a wilderness, the gait of one
Who finds no path where the path should be.

That hesitant figure, eddying away
Like a winged seed loosened from its parent stem,
Has something I never quite grasp to convey
About nature's give-and-take – the small, the scorching
Ordeals which fire one's irresolute clay.

I have had worse partings, but none that so
Gnaws at my mind still. Perhaps it is roughly
Saying what God alone could perfectly show –
How selfhood begins with a walking away,
And love is proved in the letting go.

STEPHEN SPENDER 1909–95

AN ELEMENTARY SCHOOL CLASSROOM IN A SLUM

Far far from gusty waves these children's faces.
Like rootless weeds, the hair torn round their pallor:
The tall girl with her weighed-down head. The paper-
seeming boy, with rat's eyes. The stunted, unlucky heir
Of twisted bones, reciting a father's gnarled disease,
His lesson, from his desk. At back of the dim class
One unnoted, sweet and young. His eyes live in a dream
Of squirrel's game, in tree room, other than this.

On sour cream walls, donations. Shakespeare's head,
Cloudless at dawn, civilized dome riding all cities.
Belled, flowery, Tyrolese valley. Open-handed map
Awarding the world its world. And yet, for these
Children, these windows, not this map, their world,
Where all their future's painted with a fog,
A narrow street sealed in with a lead sky
Far far from rivers, capes, and stars of words.

Surely, Shakespeare is wicked, the map a bad example,
With ships and sun and love tempting them to steal –
For lives that slyly turn in their cramped holes
From fog to endless night? On their slag heap, these children
Wear skins peeped through by bones and spectacles of steel
With mended glass, like bottle bits on stones.
All of their time and space are foggy slum.
So blot their maps with slums as big as doom.

Unless, governor, inspector, visitor,
This map becomes their window and these windows
That shut upon their lives like catacombs,
Break O break open till they break the town
And show the children to green fields, and make their world
Run azure on gold sands, and let their tongues
Run naked into books the white and green leaves open
History theirs whose language is the sun.

CHARLES CAUSLEY 1917–

───────────────

TIMOTHY WINTERS

Timothy Winters comes to school
With eyes as wide as a football-pool,
Ears like bombs and teeth like splinters:
A blitz of a boy is Timothy Winters.

His belly is white, his neck is dark,
And his hair is an exclamation-mark.
His clothes are enough to scare a crow
And through his britches the blue winds blow.

When teacher talks he won't hear a word
And he shoots down dead the arithmetic-bird,
He licks the patterns off his plate
And he's not even heard of the Welfare State.

Timothy Winters has bloody feet
And he lives in a house on Suez Street,
He sleeps in a sack on the kitchen floor
And they say there aren't boys like him any more.

Old Man Winters likes his beer
And his missus ran off with a bombardier,
Grandma sits in the grate with a gin
And Timothy's dosed with an aspirin.

The Welfare Worker lies awake
But the law's as tricky as a ten-foot snake,
So Timothy Winters drinks his cup
And slowly goes on growing up.

At Morning Prayers the Master helves
For children less fortunate than ourselves,
And the loudest response in the room is when
Timothy Winters roars 'Amen!'

So come one angel, come on ten:
Timothy Winters says 'Amen
Amen amen amen amen.'
Timothy Winters, Lord.

                                   Amen.

HOWARD NEMEROV 1920–

SEPTEMBER, THE FIRST DAY OF SCHOOL

I

My child and I hold hands on the way to school,
And when I leave him at the first-grade door
He cries a little but is brave; he does
Let go. My selfish tears remind me how
I cried before that door a life ago.
I may have had a hard time letting go.

Each fall the children must endure together
What every child also endures alone:
Learning the alphabet, the integers,
Three dozen bits and pieces of a stuff
So arbitrary, so peremptory
That worlds invisible and visible

Bow down before it, as in Joseph's dream
The sheaves bowed down and then the stars bowed down
Before the dreaming of a little boy.
That dream got him such hatred of his brothers
As cost the greater part of life to mend,
And yet great kindness came of it in the end.

II

A school is where they grind the grain of thought,
And grind the children who must mind the thought.
It may be those two grindings are but one,
As from the alphabet come Shakespeare's Plays,
As from the integers comes Euler's Law,
As from the whole, inseparably, the lives,

The shrunken lives that have not been set free
By law or by poetic phantasy.
But may they be. My child has disappeared
Behind the schoolroom door. And should I live
To see his coming forth, a life away,
I know my hope, but do not know its form

Nor hope to know it. May the fathers he finds
Among his teachers have a care of him
More than his father could. How that will look
I do not know, I do not need to know.
Even our tears belong to ritual.
But may great kindness come of it in the end.

PHILIP LARKIN 1922–85

THE SCHOOL IN AUGUST

The cloakroom pegs are empty now,
And locked the classroom door,
The hollow desks are dimmed with dust,
And slow across the floor
A sunbeam creeps between the chairs
Till the sun shines no more.

Who did their hair before this glass?
Who scratched 'Elaine loves Jill'
One drowsy summer sewing-class
With scissors on the sill?
Who practised this piano
Whose notes are now so still?

Ah, notices are taken down,
And scorebooks stowed away,
And seniors grow tomorrow
From the juniors today,
And even swimming groups can fade,
Games mistresses turn grey.

TED HUGHES 1930–98

DEAF SCHOOL

The deaf children were monkey-nimble, fish-tremulous and sudden.
Their faces were alert and simple
Like faces of little animals, small night lemurs caught in the flash-light.
They lacked a dimension,
They lacked a subtle wavering aura of sound and responses to sound.
The whole body was removed
From the vibration of air, they lived through the eyes,
The clear simple look, the instant full attention.
Their selves were not woven into a voice
Which was woven into a face
Hearing itself, its own public and audience,
An apparition in camouflage, an assertion in doubt –
Their selves were hidden, and their faces looked out of hiding.
What they spoke with was a machine,
A manipulation of fingers, a control-panel of gestures
Out there in the alien space
Separated from them –

Their unused faces were simple lenses of watchfulness
Simple pools of earnest watchfulness

Their bodies were like their hands
Nimbler than bodies, like the hammers of a piano,
A puppet agility, a simple mechanical action
A blankness of hieroglyph
A stylised lettering
Spelling out approximate signals
While the self looked through, out of the face of simple concealment
A face not merely deaf, a face in darkness, a face unaware,
A face that was simply the front skin of the self concealed and separate.

EDWARD LUCIE-SMITH 1933–

THE LESSON

'Your father's gone,' my bald headmaster said.
His shiny dome and brown tobacco jar
Splintered at once in tears. It wasn't grief.
I cried for knowledge which was bitterer
Than any grief. For there and then I knew
That grief has uses – that a father dead
Could bind the bully's fist a week or two;
And then I cried for shame, then for relief.

I was a month past ten when I learnt this:
I still remember how the noise was stilled
In school-assembly when my grief came in.
Some goldfish in a bowl quietly sculled
Around their shining prison on its shelf.
They were indifferent. All the other eyes
Were turned towards me. Somewhere in myself
Pride, like a goldfish, flashed a sudden fin.

FLEUR ADCOCK 1934–

FOR HEIDI WITH BLUE HAIR

When you dyed your hair blue
(or, at least, ultramarine
for the clipped sides, with a crest
of jet-black spikes on top)
you were sent home from school

because, as the headmistress put it,
although dyed hair was not
specifically forbidden, yours
was, apart from anything else,
not done in the school colours.

Tears in the kitchen, telephone-calls
to school from your freedom-loving father:
'She's not a punk in her behaviour;
it's just a style.' (You wiped your eyes,
also not in a school colour.)

'She discussed it with me first –
we checked the rules.' 'And anyway, Dad,
it cost twenty-five dollars.
Tell them it won't wash out –
not even if I wanted to try.'

It would have been unfair to mention
your mother's death, but that
shimmered behind the arguments.
The school had nothing else against you;
the teachers twittered and gave in.

Next day your black friend had hers done
in grey, white and flaxen yellow –
the school colours precisely:
an act of solidarity, a witty
tease. The battle was already won.

ROGER McGOUGH 1937–

FIRST DAY AT SCHOOL

A millionbillionwillion miles from home
Waiting for the bell to go. (To go where?)
Why are they all so big, other children?
So noisy? So much at home they
must have been born in uniform.
Lived all their lives in playgrounds.
Spent the years inventing games
that don't let me in. Games
that are rough, that swallow you up.

And the railings.
All around, the railings.
Are they to keep out wolves and monsters?
Things that carry off and eat children?
Things you don't take sweets from?
Perhaps they're to stop us getting out.
Running away from the lessins. Lessin.
What does a lessin look like?
Sounds small and slimy.
They keep them in glassrooms.
Whole rooms made out of glass. Imagine.

I wish I could remember my name.
Mummy said it would come in useful.
Like wellies. When there's puddles.
Yellowwellies. I wish she was here.
I think my name is sewn on somewhere.
Perhaps the teacher will read it for me.
Tea-cher. The one who makes the tea.

BRIAN PATTEN 1946–

GUST BECOS I CUD NOT SPEL

Gust becos I cud not spel
It did not mean I was daft
When the boys in school red my riting
Some of them laffed.

But now I am the dictater
They have to rite like me
Utherwise they cannot pas
Ther GCSE

Some of the girls wer ok
But those who laffed a lot
Have al bean rownded up
And hav recintly bean shot

The teecher who corrected my speling
As not been shot at al
But four the last fifteen howers
As bean standing up against a wal

He has to stand ther until he can spel
Figgymisgrugifooniyn the rite way
I think he will stand ther forever
I just inventid it today

JACKIE KAY 1961–

THE SCHOOL HAMSTER'S HOLIDAY

Remember the coal bunker in winter?
Naw? You wouldn't want to, either.
Stooping at the grate, gathering auld ash

always leaving a wee bed of ash
for the next fire's blazing dreams.
Heeking a' that heavy coal from the bunker.

The big black jewels in the steel bucket.
Toast from the naked flame was a treat,
or burning pink and white marshmallows

till they caved in and surrendered.
But that was rare.
This is what I most remember:

the time when Snowie, our school hamster,
comes home for a weekend holiday with me.
A cage is a cage no matter where the house is,

thinks Snowie, probably; so come nighttime
she escapes her prison, come nighttime
she fancies a night in a slumberdown,

climbs up the chimney breast
into the ma and da's bed.
You should have heard them scream

when they woke to see Snowie,
now the colour of soot, no snaw,
running the course of the duvet.

They were big screams, like this:
AAAAAAAAAAAAAAAAAAAAAAAAAAAAA
AAAAAAAAAAAAAAAAAAHHHHHHHHHHH

I spent the rest of the weekend
tight-lipped and desperate,
sponging that hamster with all my might

my wee yellow sponge going like a wiper,
hearing children chant in my ears,
She's made our Snowie into a darkie.

I tried and tried to make Snowie white.
It wis an impossible task.
Have you ever tried to shammy a hammy?

Monday morning wis an absolute disgrace.
I'll never forget the shame of it.
The wee GREY hamster looking po-faced.

*'This is the kind of thing I do
when I'm needing attention'*

from 'Attention Seeking'

COVENTRY PATMORE 1823–96

THE TOYS

My little son, who looked from thoughtful eyes
And moved and spoke in quiet grown-up wise,
Having my law the seventh time disobeyed,
I struck him, and dismissed
With hard words and unkissed,
His mother, who was patient, being dead.
Then, fearing lest his grief should hinder sleep,
I visited his bed,
But found him slumbering deep,
With darkened eyelids, and their lashes yet
From his late sobbing wet.
And I, with moan,
Kissing away his tears, left others of my own;
For, on a table drawn beside his head,
He had put, within his reach,
A box of counters and a red-veined stone,
A piece of glass abraded by the beach
And six or seven shells,
A bottle with bluebells
And two French copper coins, ranged there with careful art,
To comfort his sad heart.
So when that night I prayed
To God, I wept, and said:
Ah, when at last we lie with trancèd breath,
Not vexing Thee in death,
And Thou rememberest of what toys
We made our joys,
How weakly understood,
Thy great commanded good,
Then, fatherly not less
Than I whom Thou hast moulded from the clay,
Thou'lt leave Thy wrath, and say,
'I will be sorry for their childishness.'

HILAIRE BELLOC 1870–1953

MATILDA
Who told Lies, and was Burned to Death

Matilda told such Dreadful Lies,
It made one Gasp and Stretch one's Eyes;
Her Aunt, who, from her Earliest Youth,
Had kept a Strict Regard for Truth,
Attempted to Believe Matilda:
The effort very nearly killed her,
And would have done so, had not She
Discovered this Infirmity.
For once, towards the Close of Day,
Matilda, growing tired of play,
And finding she was left alone,
Went tiptoe to the Telephone
And summoned the Immediate Aid
Of London's Noble Fire-Brigade.
Within an hour the Gallant Band
Were pouring in on every hand,
From Putney, Hackney Downs, and Bow,
With Courage high and Hearts a-glow
They galloped, roaring through the Town,
'Matilda's House is Burning Down!'
Inspired by British Cheers and Loud
Proceeding from the Frenzied Crowd,
They ran their ladders through a score
Of windows on the Ball Room Floor;
And took Peculiar Pains to Souse
The Pictures up and down the House,
Until Matilda's Aunt succeeded
In showing them they were not needed;
And even then she had to pay
To get the Men to go away!

• • •

It happened that a few Weeks later

Her Aunt was off to the Theatre
To see that Interesting Play
The Second Mrs. Tanqueray.
She had refused to take her Niece
To hear this Entertaining Piece:
A Deprivation Just and Wise
To Punish her for Telling Lies.
That Night a Fire *did* break out –
You should have heard Matilda Shout!
You should have heard her Scream and Bawl,
And throw the window up and call
To People passing in the Street –
(The rapidly increasing Heat
Encouraging her to obtain
Their confidence) – but all in vain!
For every time She shouted 'Fire!'
They only answered 'Little Liar!'
And therefore when her Aunt returned,
Matilda, and the House, were Burned.

MARRIOTT EDGAR 1880–1951

THE LION AND ALBERT

There's a famous seaside place called Blackpool,
    That's noted for fresh air and fun,
And Mr and Mrs Ramsbottom
    Went there with young Albert, their son.

A grand little lad was young Albert,
    All dressed in his best; quite a swell
With a stick with an 'orse's 'ead 'andle.
    The finest that Woolworth's could sell.

They didn't think much to the Ocean:
    The waves, they was fiddlin' and small,
There was no wrecks and nobody drownded,
    Fact, nothing to laugh at at all.

So, seeking for further amusement,
    They paid and went into the Zoo,
Where they'd Lions and Tigers and Camels,
    And old ale and sandwiches too.

There was one great big Lion called Wallace;
    His nose were all covered with scars –
He lay in a somnolent posture
    With the side of his face on the bars.

Now Albert had heard about Lions,
    How they was ferocious and wild –
To see Wallace lying so peaceful,
    Well, it didn't seem right to the child.

So straightway the brave little feller,
    Not showing a morsel of fear,
Took his stick with its 'orse's 'ead 'andle
    And pushed it in Wallace's ear.

You could see that the Lion didn't like it,
    For giving a kind of a roll,
He pulled Albert inside the cage with 'im,
    And swallowed the little lad 'ole.

Then Pa, who had seen the occurrence,
    And didn't know what to do next,
Said 'Mother! Yon Lion's 'et Albert,'
    And Mother said 'Well, I am vexed!'

Then Mr and Mrs Ramsbottom –
    Quite rightly, when all's said and done –
Complained to the Animal Keeper
    That the Lion had eaten their son.

The keeper was quite nice about it;
    He said 'What a nasty mishap.
Are you sure that it's *your* boy he's eaten?'
    Pa said 'Am I sure? There's his cap!'

The manager had to be sent for.
    He came and he said 'What's to do?'
Pa said 'Yon Lion's 'et Albert,
    And 'im in his Sunday clothes, too.'

Then Mother said, 'Right's right, young feller;
    I think it's a shame and a sin
For a lion to go and eat Albert,
    And after we've paid to come in.'

The manager wanted no trouble,
    He took out his purse right away,
Saying 'How much to settle the matter?'
    And Pa said 'What do you usually pay?'

But Mother had turned a bit awkward
    When she thought where her Albert had gone,
She said 'No! someone's got to be summonsed' –
    So that was decided upon.

Then off they went to the P'lice Station,
   In front of the Magistrate chap;
They told 'im what happened to Albert,
   And proved it by showing his cap.

The Magistrate gave his opinion
   That no one was really to blame
And he said that he hoped the Ramsbottoms
   Would have further sons to their name.

At that Mother got proper blazing,
   'And thank you, sir, kindly,' said she
'What, waste all our lives raising children
   To feed ruddy Lions? Not me!'

BRIAN PATTEN 1946–

LITTLE JOHNNY'S CONFESSION

This morning
    being rather young and foolish
    I borrowed a machinegun my father
    had left hidden since the war, went out,
    and eliminated a number of small enemies.
    Since then I have not returned home.

This morning
    swarms of police with trackerdogs
    wander about the city
    with my description printed
    on their minds, asking:
    'Have you seen him?
    He is seven years old,
    likes Pluto, Mighty Mouse
    and Biffo the Bear,
    have you seen him, anywhere?'

This morning
    sitting alone in a strange playground
    muttering you've blundered, you've blundered
    over and over to myself
    I work out my next move
    but cannot move.
    The trackerdogs will sniff me out,
    they have my lollypops.

JACKIE KAY 1961–

ATTENTION SEEKING

I'm needing attention.
I know I'm needing attention
because I hear people say it.
People that know these things.
I'm needing attention,
so what I'll do is steal something.
I know I'll steal something
because that is what I do
when I'm needing attention.
Or else I'll mess up my sister's room,
throw all her clothes onto the floor,
put her gerbil under her pillow
and lay a trap above the door
a big heavy dictionary to drop on her
when she comes through. (Swot.)
This is the kind of thing I do
when I'm needing attention.
But I'm never boring.
I always think up new things.
Attention has lots of colours
and tunes. And lots of punishments.
For attention you can get detention.
Extra homework. Extra housework.
All sorts of things. Although
yesterday I heard the woman say
that I was just needing
someone to listen. My dad went mad.
'Listen to him!' he said. 'Listen!
You've got to be joking.'
Mind you that was right after
I stole his car keys and drove
his car straight into the wall.
I wasn't hurt, but I'm still
needing quite a lot of attention.

'*When my silent terror cried,*
Nobody, nobody replied'

from 'Autobiography'

BEN JONSON 1572–1637

ON MY FIRST SON

Farewell, thou child of my right hand, and joy;
    My sin was too much hope of thee, loved boy.
Seven years thou wert lent to me, and I thee pay,
    Exacted by thy fate, on the just day.

Oh, could I lose all father now! For why
    Will man lament the state he should envy?
To have so soon 'scaped world's and flesh's rage,
    And, if no other misery, yet age?
Rest in soft peace, and, asked, say here doth lie
    Ben Johnson his best piece of poetry;
For whose sake, henceforth, all his vows be such,
    As what he loves may never like too much.

ON MY FIRST DAUGHTER

Here lies to each her parents' ruth
Mary, the daughter of their youth:
Yet, all Heaven's gifts being Heaven's due,
It makes the father less to rue.
At six months' end she parted hence
With safety of her innocence;
Whose soul Heaven's Queen (whose name she bears)
In comfort of her mother's tears,
Hath placed amongst her virgin-train;
Where, while that severed doth remain,
This grave partakes the fleshly birth,
Which cover lightly, gentle earth.

WILLIAM BLAKE 1757–1827

HOLY THURSDAY (I)

'Twas on a Holy Thursday, their innocent faces clean,
The children walking two & two, in red & blue & green,
Grey headed beadles walkd before with wands as white as snow,
Till into the high dome of Paul's they like Thames' waters flow.

O what a multitude they seemd, these flowers of London town!
Seated in companies they sit with radiance all their own.
The hum of multitudes was there, but multitudes of lambs.
Thousands of little boys & girls raising their innocent hands.

Now like a mighty wind they raise to heaven the voice of song,
Or like harmonious thunderings the seats of heaven among.
Beneath them sit the aged men, wise guardians of the poor;
Then cherish pity, lest you drive an angel from your door.

WILLIAM BLAKE 1757–1827

HOLY THURSDAY (II)

Is this a holy thing to see,
In a rich and fruitful land,
Babes reduced to misery,
Fed with cold and usurous hand?

Is that trembling cry a song?
Can it be a song of joy?
And so many children poor?
It is a land of poverty!

And their sun does never shine,
And their fields and bleak & bare,
And their ways are fill'd with thorns;
It is eternal winter there.

For where-e'er the sun does shine,
And where-e'er the rain does fall,
Babe can never hunger there,
Nor poverty the mind appall.

FELICIA HEMANS 1793–1835

CASABIANCA

The boy stood on the burning deck
    Whence all but he had fled;
The flame that lit the battle's wreck
    Shone round him o'er the dead.

Yet beautiful and bright he stood,
    As born to rule the storm –
A creature of heroic blood,
    A proud, though childlike form.

The flames rolled on – he would not go
    Without his father's word;
That father, faint in death below,
    His voice no longer heard.

He called aloud: 'Say, father, say
    If yet my task is done!'
He knew not that the chieftain lay
    Unconscious of his son.

'Speak, father!' once again he cried,
    'If I may yet be gone!'
And but the booming shots replied,
    And fast the flames rolled on.

Upon his brow he felt their breath,
    And in his waving hair,
And looked from that lone post of death
    In still yet brave despair:

And shouted but once more aloud,
    'My father! must I stay?'
While o'er him fast, through sail and shroud,
    The wreathing fires made way.

They wrapt the ship in splendour wild,
   They caught the flag on high.
And streamed above the gallant child
   Like banners in the sky.

There came a burst of thunder-sound –
   The boy – oh! where was he?
Ask of the winds that far around
   With fragments strewed the sea! –

With mast, and helm, and pennon fair,
   That well had borne their part;
But the noblest thing which perished there
   Was that young faithful heart!

ELIZABETH BARRETT BROWNING 1806–61

from THE CRY OF THE CHILDREN
'Alas, alack, why do ye gaze upon me with your eyes, my children?'
Euripides, *Medea.*

Do ye hear the children weeping, O my brothers,
    Ere the sorrow comes with years?
They are leaning their young heads against their mothers,
    And *that* cannot stop their tears.
The young lambs are bleating in the meadows;
    The young birds are chirping in the nest;
The young fawns are playing with the shadows;
    The young flowers are blowing toward the west —
But the young, young children, O my brothers,
    They are weeping bitterly!
They are weeping in the playtime of the others,
    In the country of the free.

Do you question the young children in the sorrow,
    Why their tears are falling so? —
The old man may weep for his to-morrow
    Which is lost in Long Ago —
The old tree is leafless in the forest —
    The old year is ending in the frost —
The old wound, if stricken, is the sorest —
    The old hope is hardest to be lost;
But the young, young children, O my brothers,
    Do you ask them why they stand
Weeping sore before the bosoms of their mothers,
    In our happy Fatherland!

They look up with their pale and sunken faces,
    And their looks are sad to see,
For the man's grief abhorrent draws and presses
    Down the cheeks of infancy.
'Your old earth,' they say, 'is very dreary';
    'Our young feet,' they say, 'are very weak!
Few paces have we taken, yet are weary —

Our grave-rest is very far to seek!
Ask the aged why they weep, and not the children;
   For the outside earth is cold, —
And we young ones stand without, in our bewildering,
   And the graves are for the old.'

'True,' say the children, 'it may happen
   That we die before our time!
Little Alice died last year — the grave is shapen
   Like a snowball, in the rime.
We looked into the pit prepared to take her —
   Was no room for any work in the close clay!
From the sleep wherein she lieth none will wake her,
   Crying, "Get up, little Alice! it is day."
If you listen by that grave, in sun and shower,
   With your ear down, little Alice never cries! —
Could we see her face, be sure we should not know her,
   For the smile has time for growing in her eyes:
And merry go her moments, lulled and stilled in
    The shroud, by the kirk-chime!
It is good when it happens,' say the children,
   'That we die before our time!'

HERBERT READ 1893–1968

BOMBING CASUALTIES: SPAIN

Dolls' faces are rosier but these were children
their eyes not glass but gleaming gristle
dark lenses in whose quicksilvery glances
the sunlight quivered. These blenched lips
were warm once and bright with blood
but blood
held in a moist bleb of flesh
not spilt and spatter'd in tousled hair.

In these shadowy tresses
red petals did not always
thus clot and blacken to a scar.

These are dead faces:
wasps' nests are not more wanly waxen
wood embers not so greyly ashen.

They are laid out in ranks
like paper lanterns that have fallen
after a night of riot
extinct in the dry morning air.

LOUIS MACNEICE 1907–63

AUTOBIOGRAPHY

In my childhood trees were green
And there was plenty to be seen.

Come back early or never come.

My father made the walls resound,
He wore his collar the wrong way round.

Come back early or never come.

My mother wore a yellow dress;
Gently, gently, gentleness.

Come back early or never come.

When I was five the black dreams came;
Nothing after was quite the same.

Come back early or never come.

The dark was talking to the dead;
The lamp was dark beside my bed.

Come back early or never come.

When I woke they did not care;
Nobody, nobody was there.

Come back early or never come.

When my silent terror cried,
Nobody, nobody replied.

Come back early or never come.

I got up; the chilly sun
Saw me walk away alone.

Come back early or never come.

ELIZABETH BISHOP 1911–79

SQUATTER'S CHILDREN

On the unbreathing sides of hills
they play, a specklike girl and boy,
alone, but near a specklike house.
The sun's suspended eye
blinks casually, and then they wade
gigantic waves of light and shade.
A dancing yellow spot, a pup,
attends them. Clouds are piling up;

a storm piles up behind the house.
The children play at digging holes.
The ground is hard; they try to use
one of their father's tools,
a mattock with a broken haft
the two of them can scarcely lift.
It drops and clangs. Their laughter spreads
effulgence in the thunderheads,

weak flashes of inquiry
direct as is the puppy's bark.
But to their little, soluble,
unwarrantable ark,
apparently the rain's reply
consists of echolalia,
and Mother's voice, ugly as sin,
keeps calling to them to come in.

Children, the threshold of the storm
has slid beneath your muddy shoes;
wet and beguiled, you stand among
the mansions you may choose
out of a bigger house than yours,
whose unlawfulness endures.
Its soggy documents retain
your rights in rooms of falling rain.

JON SILKIN 1930–97

DEATH OF A SON
(who died in a mental hospital aged one)

Something has ceased to come along with me.
Something like a person: something very like one.
And there was no nobility in it
Or anything like that.

Something was there like a one year
Old house, dumb as stone. While the near buildings
Sang like birds and laughed
Understanding the pact

They were to have with silence. But he
Neither sang nor laughed. He did not bless silence
Like bread, with words.
He did not forsake silence.

But rather, like a house in mourning
Kept the eye turned in to watch the silence while
The other houses like birds
Sang around him.

And the breathing silence neither
Moved nor was still.

I have seen stones: I have seen brick
But this house was made up of neither bricks nor stone
But a house of flesh and blood
With flesh of stone

And bricks for blood. A house
Of stones and blood in breathing silence with the other
Birds singing crazy on its chimneys.
But this was silence,

This was something else, this was
Hearing and speaking though he was a house drawn
Into silence, this was
Something religious in his silence.

Something shining in his quiet,
This was different this was altogether something else:
Though he never spoke, this
Was something to do with death.

And then slowly the eye stopped looking
Inward. The silence rose and became still.
The look turned to the outer place and stopped,
With the birds still shrilling around him.
And as if he could speak

He turned over on his side with his one year
Red as a wound
He turned over as if he could be sorry for this
And out of his eyes two great tears rolled, like
stones, and he died.

SEAMUS HEANEY 1939–

MID-TERM BREAK

I sat all morning in the college sick bay
Counting bells knelling classes to a close.
At two o'clock our neighbours drove me home.

In the porch I met my father crying –
He had always taken funerals in his stride –
And Big Jim Evans saying it was a hard blow.

The baby cooed and laughed and rocked the pram
When I came in, and I was embarrassed
By old men standing up to shake my hand

And tell me they were 'sorry for my trouble'.
Whispers informed strangers I was the eldest,
Away at school, as my mother held my hand

In hers and coughed out angry tearless sighs.
At ten o'clock the ambulance arrived
With the corpse, stanched and bandaged by the nurses.

Next morning I went up into the room. Snowdrops
And candles soothed the bedside. I saw him
For the first time in six weeks. Paler now,

Wearing a poppy bruise on his left temple,
He lay in the four foot box as in his cot.
No gaudy scars, the bumper knocked him clear.

A four foot box, a foot for every year.

WENDY COPE 1945–

TICH MILLER

Tich Miller wore glasses
with elastoplast-pink frames
and had one foot three sizes larger than the other.

When they picked teams for outdoor games
she and I were always the last two
left standing by the wire-mesh fence.

We avoided one another's eyes,
stooping, perhaps, to re-tie a shoelace,
or affecting interest in the flight

of some fortunate bird, and pretended
not to hear the urgent conference:
'Have Tubby!' 'No, no, have Tich!'

Usually they chose me, the lesser dud,
and she lolloped, unselected,
to the back of the other team.

At eleven we went to different schools.
In time I learned to get my own back,
sneering at hockey-players who couldn't spell.

Tich died when she was twelve.

'You grow like a beanstalk
as tall as a tale'

from 'You Grow like a Beanstalk'

WILLIAM WORDSWORTH 1770–1850

---

from THE PRELUDE

SKATING

     — All shod with steel,
We hiss'd along the polish'd ice, in games
Confederate, imitative of the chace
And woodland pleasures, the resounding horn,
The Pack loud bellowing, and the hunted hare.
So through the darkness and the cold we flew,
And not a voice was idle; with the din,
Meanwhile, the precipices rang aloud,
The leafless trees, and every icy crag
Tinkled like iron, while the distant hills
Into the tumult sent an alien sound
Of melancholy, not unnoticed, while the stars,
Eastward, were sparkling clear, and in the west
The orange sky of evening died away.

 Not seldom from the uproar I retired
Into a silent bay, or sportively
Glanced sideway, leaving the tumultous throng,
To cut across the image of a star
That gleam'd upon the ice: and oftentimes
When we had given our bodies to the wind,
And all the shadowy banks, on either side,
Came sweeping through the darkness, spinning still
The rapid line of motion; then at once
Have I, reclining back upon my heels,
Stopp'd short, yet still the solitary Cliffs
Wheeled by me, even as if the earth had roll'd
With visible motion her diurnal round;
Behind me did they stretch in solemn train
Feebler and feebler, and I stood and watch'd
Till all was tranquil as a dreamless sleep.

H. W. LONGFELLOW 1807–82

THE CHILDREN'S HOUR

Between the dark and the daylight,
    When the night is beginning to
        lower,
Comes a pause in the day's
        occupations,
    That is known as the Children's
        Hour.

I hear in the chamber above me
    The patter of little feet,
The sound of a door that is opened,
    And voices soft and sweet.

From my study I see in the
        lamplight,
    Descending the broad hall stair,
Grave Alice, and laughing Allegra,
    And Edith with golden hair.

A whisper, and then a silence:
    Yet I know by their merry eyes
They are plotting and planning
        together
    To take me by surprise.

A sudden rush from the stairway,
    A sudden raid from the hall!
By three doors left unguarded,
    They enter my castle wall!

They climb up into my turret
    O'er the arms and back of my
        chair;
If I try to escape, they surround me;
    They seem to be everywhere.

They almost devour me with kisses,
   Their arms about me entwine,
Till I think of the Bishop of Bingen
   In his Mouse-Tower on the Rhine!

Do you think, O blue-eyed banditti,
   Because you have scaled the wall,
Such an old moustache as I am
   Is not a match for you all?

I have you fast in my fortress,
   And will not let you depart,
But put you down into the dungeon
   In the round-tower of my heart.

And there I shall keep you forever,
   Yes, forever and a day,
Till the walls shall crumble to ruin,
   And moulder in dust away!

H. W. LONGFELLOW 1807–82

from THE SONG OF HIAWATHA

III. HIAWATHA'S CHILDHOOD

By the shores of Gitche Gumee,
By the shining Big-Sea-Water,
Stood the wigwam of Nokomis,
Daughter of the Moon, Nokomis.
Dark behind it rose the forest,
Rose the black and gloomy pine-trees,
Rose the firs with cones upon them;
Bright before it beat the water,
Beat the clear and sunny water,
Beat the shining Big-Sea-Water.
    There the wrinkled, old Nokomis
Nursed the little Hiawatha,
Rocked him in his linden cradle,
Bedded soft in moss and rushes,
Safely bound with reindeer sinews;
Stilled his fretful wail by saying,
'Hush! the Naked Bear will hear thee!'
Lulled him into slumber, singing,
'Ewa-yea! my little owlet!
Who is this, that lights the wigwam?
With his great eyes lights the wigwam?
Ewa-yea! my little owlet!'
    Many things Nokomis taught him
Of the stars that shine in heaven;
Showed him Ishkoodah, the comet,
Ishkoodah, with fiery tresses;
Showed the Death-Dance of the spirits,
Warriors with their plumes and war-clubs,
Flaring far away to northward
In the frosty nights of Winter;
Showed the broad, white road in heaven,
Pathway of the ghosts, the shadows,

Running straight across the heavens,
Crowded with the ghosts, the shadows.
   At the door on summer evenings
Sat the little Hiawatha;
Heard the whispering of the pine-trees,
Heard the lapping of the water,
Sounds of music, words of wonder:
'Minne-wawa!' said the pine-trees,
'Mudway-aushka!' said the water.
   Saw the fire-fly, Wah-wah-taysee,
Flitting through the dusk of evening,
With the twinkle of its candle
Lighting up the brakes and bushes;
And he sang the song of children,
Sang the song Nokomis taught him:
'Wah-wah-taysee, little fire-fly,
Little, flitting, white-fire insect,
Little, dancing, white-fire creature,
Light me with your little candle,
Ere upon my bed I lay me,
Ere in sleep I close my eyelids!'
   Saw the moon rise from the water
Rippling, rounding from the water,
Saw the flecks and shadows on it,
Whispered, 'What is that, Nokomis?'
And the good Nokomis answered:
'Once a warrior, very angry,
Seized his grandmother, and threw her
Up into the sky at midnight;
Right against the moon he threw her;
'Tis her body that you see there.'
   Saw the rainbow in the heaven,

In the eastern sky, the rainbow,
Whispered, 'What is that, Nokomis?'
And the good Nokomis answered:
''Tis the heaven of flowers you see there;
All the wild-flowers of the forest,
All the lilies of the prairie,
When on earth they fade and perish,
Blossom in that heaven above us.'
   When he heard the owls at midnight,
Hooting, laughing in the forest,
'What is that?' he cried in terror;
'What is that?' he said, 'Nokomis?'
And the good Nokomis answered:
'That is but the owl and owlet,
Talking in their native language,
Talking, scolding at each other.'
   Then the little Hiawatha
Learned of every bird its language,
Learned their names and all their secrets,
How they built their nests in Summer,
Where they hid themselves in Winter,
Talked with them whene'er he met them,
Called them 'Hiawatha's Chickens'.
Of all beasts he learned the language,
Learned their names and all their secrets,
How the beavers built their lodges,
Where the squirrels hid their acorns,
How the reindeer ran so swiftly,
Why the rabbit was so timid,
Talked with them whene'er he met them,
Called them 'Hiawatha's Brothers'.

ROBERT LOUIS STEVENSON 1850–94

THE LAMPLIGHTER

My tea is nearly ready and the sun has left the sky;
It's time to take the window to see Leerie going by;
For every night at teatime and before you take your seat,
With lantern and with ladder he comes posting up the street.

Now Tom would be a driver and Maria go to sea,
And my papa's a banker and as rich as he can be;
But I, when I am stronger and can choose what I'm to do,
O Leerie, I'll go round at night and light the lamps with you!

For we are very lucky, with a lamp before the door,
And Leerie stops to light it as he lights so many more;
And O! before you hurry by with ladder and with light,
O Leerie, see a little child and nod to him to-night!

LAURENCE BINYON 1869–1943

THE LITTLE DANCERS

Lonely, save for a few faint stars, the sky
Dreams; and lonely, below, the little street
Into its gloom retires, secluded and shy.
Scarcely the dumb roar enters this soft retreat:
And all is dark, save where come flooding rays
From a tavern-window; there, to the brisk measure
Of an organ that down in an alley merrily plays,
Two children, all alone and no one by,
Holding their tattered frocks, thro' an airy maze
Of motion lightly threaded with nimble feet
Dance sedately; face to face they gaze,
Their eyes shining, grave with a perfect pleasure.

A. A. MILNE 1882–1956

BUCKINGHAM PALACE

They're changing guard at Buckingham Palace –
Christopher Robin went down with Alice.
Alice is marrying one of the guard.
'A soldier's life is terrible hard,'
                    Says Alice.

They're changing guard at Buckingham Palace –
Christopher Robin went down with Alice.
We saw a guard in a sentry-box.
'One of the sergeants looks after their socks,'
                    Says Alice.

They're changing guard at Buckingham Palace –
Christopher Robin went down with Alice.
We looked for the King, but he never came.
'Well, God take care of him, all the same,'
                    Says Alice.

They're changing guard at Buckingham Palace –
Christopher Robin went down with Alice.
They've great big parties inside the grounds.
'I wouldn't be King for a hundred pounds,'
                    Says Alice.

They're changing guard at Buckingham Palace –
Christopher Robin went down with Alice.
A face looked out, but it wasn't the King's.
'He's much too busy a-signing things,'
                    Says Alice.

They're changing guard at Buckingham Palace –
Christopher Robin went down with Alice.
'Do you think the King knows all about *me*?'
'*Sure to*, dear, but it's time for tea,'
                    Says Alice.

EDWIN MUIR 1887–1959

CHILDHOOD

Long time he lay upon the sunny hill,
    To his father's house below securely bound.
Far off the silent, changing sound was still,
    With the black islands lying thick around.

He saw each separate height, each vaguer hue,
    Where the massed islands rolled in mist away,
And though all ran together in his view
    He knew that unseen straits between them lay.

Often he wondered what new shores were there.
    In thought he saw the still light on the sand,
The shallow water clear in tranquil air,
    And walked through it in joy from strand to strand.

Over the sound a ship so slow would pass
    That in the black hill's gloom it seemed to lie.
The evening sound was smooth like sunken glass,
    And time seemed finished ere the ship passed by.

Gray tiny rocks slept round him where he lay,
    Moveless as they, more still as evening came,
The grasses threw straight shadows far away,
    And from the house his mother called his name.

SIR JOHN BETJEMAN 1906–84

HUNTER TRIALS

It's awf'lly bad luck on Diana,
   Her ponies have swallowed their bits;
She fished down their throats with a spanner
   And frightened them all into fits.

So now she's attempting to borrow.
   Do lend her some bits, Mummy, *do*;
I'll lend her my own for to-morrow,
   But to-day *I*'ll be wanting them too.

Just look at Prunella on Guzzle,
   The wizardest pony on earth;
Why doesn't she slacken his muzzle
   And tighten the breech in his girth?

I say, Mummy, there's Mrs Geyser
   And doesn't she look pretty sick?
I bet it's because Mona Lisa
   Was hit on the hock with a brick.

Miss Blewitt says Monica threw it,
   But Monica says it was Joan,
And Joan's very thick with Miss Blewitt,
   So Monica's sulking alone.

And Margaret failed in her paces,
   Her withers got tied in a noose,
So her coronets caught in the traces
   And now all her fetlocks are loose.

Oh, it's me now. I'm terribly nervous.
   I wonder if Smudges will shy.
She's practically certain to swerve as
   Her Pelham is over one eye.

* * *

Oh wasn't it naughty of Smudges?
   Oh, Mummy, I'm sick with disgust.
She threw me in front of the Judges,
   And my silly old collarbone's bust.

SÉAN RAFFERTY 1909–93

'YOU GROW LIKE A BEANSTALK'

You grow like a beanstalk
as tall as a tale;
twining your time a garland, the leaves are all
shaped in a single heart, to climb until
you stand as high as your wish and what's over the wall
flowers in your eye, a marvel, to teach the tongue
the scale of tomorrow and elsewhere. The song to be sung.

Once, o legends ago,
in the halfway house
by the fire where bedward candles beg their flame
I read you the tale of the thumb-tall girl who was swept
away on a lily leaf, the toad, the mouse;
you so still on my lap I thought you slept.
But the story darkened. The mole's long galleries came
nowhere to guess or glimmer of ending: grief.
Tears that would not, would not be comforted, no
though the risen bird was king and south was home
would not: away on a woman's tears far past belief
in a happy ever and after I watched you go
Ceres in search of her child a child gone down to the dark.
I heard you a woman cry
and born a maiden you wept for the maidens who die.

Soon I listen
and you, the traveller, make
plans for an early start; your turn to tell
the other side of the story. The path you take
is worn like a wish: beasts are clumsy and kind
the birds are concerned about orphans, nothing has changed, the
    lake
copies its only landscape of turrets and trees, you find
the house they told you was ruined and there at last
the sun is taking the girl in her bridal dress,

96

the six white horses are waiting, across the park
bells are rising, immaculate doves fly past
over your future and after them into the dark
my fears go up like fireworks, salute and bless
as far as a wish can see or a heart can guess.

ELIZABETH BISHOP 1911–79

SESTINA

September rain falls on the house.
In the failing light, the old grandmother
sits in the kitchen with the child
beside the Little Marvel Stove,
reading the jokes from the almanac,
laughing and talking to hide her tears.

She thinks that her equinoctial tears
and the rain that beats on the roof of the house
were both foretold by the almanac,
but only known to a grandmother.
The iron kettle sings on the stove.
She cuts some bread and says to the child,

It's time for tea now; but the child
is watching the teakettle's small hard tears
dance like mad on the hot black stove,
the way the rain must dance on the house.
Tidying up, the old grandmother
hangs up the clever almanac

on its string. Birdlike, the almanac
hovers half open above the child,
hovers above the old grandmother
and her teacup full of dark brown tears.
She shivers and says she thinks the house
feels chilly, and puts more wood in the stove.

It was to be, says the Marvel Stove.
I know what I know, says the almanac.
With crayons the child draws a rigid house
and a winding pathway. Then the child
puts in a man with buttons like tears
and shows it proudly to the grandmother.

But secretly, while the grandmother
busies herself about the stove,
the little moons fall down like tears
from between the pages of the almanac
into the flower bed the child
has carefully placed in the front of the house.

Time to plant tears, says the almanac.
The grandmother sings to the marvellous stove
and the child draws another inscrutable house.

JOHN CASSIDY 1928–

FROZEN CANAL

After three days of frost a boy on a bike
Is daringly first to prove the black

Top of the iced canal a highway now,
Slick between banks off-white with old snow.

Dodging a bottle buried to its snout
And an iceberg tyre one-ninth out

He spins with an Indian whoop under a bridge
Past his companions fringing the timid edge,

And they follow, all of them, to ride and skitter and glide
Along the hissing crown of this new road.

Then a heavy drumming in the frosted air
Brings the butting shoulders of the ice-breaker,

The spoil-sport barge labouring to thump and crack
Leaving brick-sized ice-blocks jumbled in its wake.

Deliberate this. Under unreflecting ice
The sepia water waits for a shocked face

To splinter and blunder in, waits for a mouth
It can fill with sludge to silence, throttling the breath.

It happens – often enough for a barge to be sent
Whenever the ice will hold a footstep, blunt

Prow pushing the games away to the thrum
Of diesels. The boys stand with their beached bike, dumb

Till the devastating passage has rumbled through,
Then shrilling at the helmsman, hurling futile snow.

But he, indifferent, steers on his ordered track,
While they, saved, desolated, swear at his crouched back.

CAROL ANN DUFFY 1955–

CHOCS

Into the half-pound box of Moonlight
my small hand crept.
There was an electrifying rustle.
There was a dark and glamorous scent.
Into my open, moist mouth
the first Montelimar went.

Down in the crinkly second layer,
five finger-piglets snuffled
among the Hazelnut Whirl,
the Caramel Square,
the Black Cherry and Almond Truffle.

Bliss.

I chomped. I gorged.
I stuffed my face,
till only the Coffee Cream
was left for the owner of the box –
tough luck, Anne Pope –
oh, and half an Orange Supreme.

JACKIE KAY 1961–

GOING TO SEE *KING LEAR*

On the big red smooth seat, I
watch the giant television
and my mother's eyes, greedy,
gulping everything down like
chocolate raisins. In front
of me are rows of heads that
put me in such a bad mood:

sleek shining page-boy, snobby
at the back; tight bossy bun,
trapped in a net; tall, selfish
beehive blocking my view. Then,
all of a sudden, darkness
comes down, sweet, and will not melt
in the hand or in the mouth.

I am sitting with strangers,
just the shapes and silhouettes
of them now. We breath in, all
of us, in one breath waiting
to be changed, to stop time or
for the trailer to end and
King Lear begin. No children,

except me, watching with mum,
who leans forward, her body,
diagonal, her fury
at good King Lear's disloyal
daughters, she whispers, 'Get out'
to the good one, Or 'Don't put
up with that.' (I think it was
Cordelia.) When King Lear's
Gloucester gets his eyes gouged out,
my mother falls off her chair.

I cover my eyes. Too late.
I've seen it. The terrible
tormenting sight of a man's
hands over his helpless, scooped

sockets, staggering back to
some other time of trust, whilst
those egg-whites of his eyes run.
'Vile jelly,' I shake, appalled.
Lear foams, whisked-white, at the mouth.
Jesus, my mother says, shocked,
That was good. That was so good.

Her eyes glint, green with pleasure.
Deep sigh when the names appear
and disappear. So slowly,
she rises from the red seat.
I had to see it. I did.
What a good, good girl, sitting
all quiet. My mouth has fallen

open for good. It won't close.
I am seven, I have seen
Lear's best friend get his eyes poked
out. The red floor is sliding
downwards. I will fall into
myself years later; grown-up,
velvet curtains drawn open.

'Seven years old; he made up novels: life
In the desert, Liberty in transports gleaming,
Forests, suns, shores, swamps'

from 'Seven-Year-Old Poets'

WILLIAM BLAKE 1757–1827

from SONGS OF INNOCENCE

INTRODUCTION

Piping down the valleys wild
Piping songs of pleasant glee
On a cloud I saw a child,
And he laughing said to me,

'Pipe a song about a Lamb';
So I piped with merry chear.
'Piper pipe that song again' –
So I piped, he wept to hear.

'Drop thy pipe thy happy pipe
Sing thy songs of happy cheer';
So I sung the same again
While he wept with joy to hear.

'Piper sit thee down and write
In a book that all may read' –
So he vanish'd from my sight.
And I pluck'd a hollow reed,

And I made a rural pen,
And I stain'd the water clear,
And I wrote my happy songs
Every child may joy to hear.

ROBERT LOUIS STEVENSON 1850–94

CHILDREN

Swinging in a palanquin;
Where among the desert sands
Some deserted city stands,
All its children, sweep and prince,
Grown to manhood ages since,
Not a foot in street or house,
Not a stir of child or mouse,
And when kindly falls the night,
In all the town no spark of light.
There I'll come when I'm a man
With a camel caravan;
Light a fire in the gloom
Of some dusty dining-room;
See the pictures on the walls,
Heroes, fights and festivals;
And in a corner find the toys
Of the old Egyptian boys.

ROBERT LOUIS STEVENSON 1850–94

THE LAND OF COUNTERPANE

I was the giant great and still
That sits upon the pillow-hill,
And sees before him, dale and plain,
The pleasant land of counterpane.

ARTHUR RIMBAUD 1854–91

SEVEN-YEAR-OLD POETS

The Mother closed the copybook, and went away
Content, and very proud, and never saw
In the blue eyes, beneath the pimply forehead,
The horror and loathing in her child's soul.

All day he sweat obedience; was very
Bright; still, some black tics, some traits he had
Seemed to foreshadow sour hypocrisies.
In the dark halls, their mildewed paper peeling,
He passed, stuck out his tongue, then pressed two fists
In his crotch, and shut his eyes to see spots.

A door opened: in the evening lamplight
There he was, gasping on the banisters
In a well of light that hung beneath the roof.
Summer especially, stupid, slow, he always tried
To shut himself up in the cool latrine,
There he could think, be calm, and sniff the air.

Washed from the smells of day, the garden, in winter,
Out behind the house, filled with moonlight;
Stretched below a wall, and rolled in dirt,
Squeezing his dazzled eyes to make visions come,
He only heard the scruffy fruit trees grow.
A pity! The friends he had were puny kids,
The ones with runny eyes that streaked their cheeks,
Who hid thin yellow fingers, smeared with mud,
Beneath old cast-off clothes that stank of shit;
They used to talk like gentle idiots.
If she surprised him in these filthy friendships
His mother grew afraid; the child's deep tenderness
Took her astonishment to task. How good . . .
Her wide blue eyes – but they lie.

Seven years old; he made up novels: life
In the desert, Liberty in transports gleaming,
Forests, suns, shores, swamps! Inspiration
In picture magazines: he looked, red-faced,
At Spanish and Italian girls who laughed.
And when, with brown eyes, wild, in calico,
 – She was eight – the workers' girl next door
Played rough, jumped right on top of him
In a corner, onto his back, and pulled his hair,
And he was under her, he bit her ass
Because she wore no panties underneath;
Then, beaten by her, hit with fists and heels,
He took the smell of her skin back to his room.

He hated pale December Sunday afternoons:
With plastered hair, on a mahogany couch,
He read the cabbage-coloured pages of a Bible;
Dreams oppressed him every night in bed.

He hated God, but loved the men he saw
Returning home in dirty working clothes
Through the wild evening air to the edge of town,
Where criers, rolling drums before the edicts,
Made the crowds around them groan and laugh.
 – He dreamed of prairies of love, where shining herds,
Perfumes of life, pubescent stalks of gold
Swirled slowly round, and then rose up and flew.

The darkest things in life could move him most;
When in that empty room, the shutters closed,
High and blue, with its bitter humid smell,
He read his novel – always on his mind –
Full of heavy ochre skies and drowning forests,

Flowers of flesh in starry woods uncurled,
Catastrophe, vertigo, pity and disaster!
 – While the noises of the neighbourhood swelled
Below – stretched out alone on unbleached
Canvas sheets, a turbulent vision of sails!

WALTER DE LA MARE 1873–1956

THE CHILDREN OF STARE

Winter is fallen early
On the house of Stare;
Birds in reverberating flocks
Haunt its ancestral box;
Bright are the plenteous berries
In clusters in the air.

Still is the fountain's music,
The dark pool icy still,
Whereupon a small and sanguine sun
Floats in a mirror on,
Into a West of crimson,
From a South of daffodil.

'Tis strange to see young children
In such a wintry house;
Like rabbits' on the frozen snow
Their tell-tale footprints go;
Their laughter rings like timbrels
'Neath evening ominous:

Their small and heightened faces
Like wine-red winter buds;
Their frolic bodies gentle as
Flakes in the air that pass,
Frail as the twirling petal
From the briar of the woods.

Above them silence lours,
Still as an arctic sea;
Light fails; night falls; the wintry moon
Glitters; the crocus soon
Will open grey and distracted
On earth's austerity:

Thick mystery, wild peril,
Law like an iron rod: –
Yet sport they on in Spring's attire,
Each with his tiny fire
Blown to a core of ardour
By the awful breath of God.

W.J. TURNER 1889–1946

ROMANCE

When I was but thirteen or so
　　I went into a golden land;
Chimborazo, Cotopaxi
　　Took me by the hand.

My father died, my brother too,
　　They passed like fleeting dreams,
I stood where Popocatapetl
　　In the sunlight gleams.

I dimly heard the master's voice
　　And boys far off at play;
Chimborazo, Copotaxi
　　Had stolen me away.

I walked in a great golden dream
　　To and fro from school –
Shining Popocatapetl
　　The dusty streets did rule.

I walked home with a gold dark boy
　　And never a word I'd say;
Chimborazo, Cotopaxi
　　Had taken my speech away:

I gazed entranced upon his face
　　Fairer than any flower –
O shining Popocatapetl,
　　It was thy magic hour:

The houses, people, traffic seemed
　　Thin fading dreams by day;
Chimborazo, Cotopaxi,
　　They had stolen my soul away!

JOSEPHINE JACOBSEN 1908–

THE PRIMER

I said in my youth
'they lie to children'
but it is not so.
Mother my goose I know
told me the truth.

I remember that treetop minute.
That was a baby is a woman now:
in a rough wind, it was a broken bough
brought down the cradle with the baby in it.

I had a dumpy friend (you would not know his name,
though he indeed had several), after his fall
lay in live pieces by my garden wall
in a vain tide of epaulettes and manes.

I had another friend (and you would know her name),
took up her candle on her way to bed.
She had a steady hand and a yellow head
up the tall stairwell, but the chopper came.

So small they meant to run away, from sightless eyes
three mice ran toward my mind instead;
I seized the shapely knife. They fled
in scarlet haste, the blind and tailless mice.

Cock robin was three birds of a single feather.
Three times cock robin fell when a breeze blew;
eye of fly watched; arrow of sparrow flew:
three times cock robin died in the same weather.

Sheep, cows, meander in the corn and meadow;
soundless the horn, fine, fine my seam;
nothing I feed, but rosy grows my cream.
My blue boy sleeps under the stack's huge shadow.

RANDALL JARRELL 1914–65

A SICK CHILD

The postman comes when I am still in bed.
'Postman, what do you have for me today?'
I say to him. (But really I'm in bed.)
Then he says – what shall I have him say?

'This letter says that you are president
Of – this word here; it's a republic.'
Tell them I can't answer right away.
'It's your duty.' No, I'd rather just be sick.

Then he tells me there are letters saying everything
That I can think of that I want for them to say.
I say, 'Well, thank you very much. Good-bye.'
He is ashamed, and turns and walks away.

If I can think of it, it isn't what I want.
I want . . . I want a ship from some near star
To land in the yard, and beings to come out
And think to me: 'So this is where you are!

Come,' Except that they won't do,
I thought of them. . . . And yet somewhere there must be
Something that's different from everything.
All that I've never thought of – think of me!

TONY CONNOR 1930–

A CHILD HALF-ASLEEP

Stealthily parting the small-hours silence,
a hardly-embodied figment of his brain
comes down to sit with me
as I work late.
Flat-footed, as though his legs and feet
were still asleep.

He sits on a stool,
staring into the fire,
his dummy dangling.

Fire ignites the small coals of his eyes.
It stares back through the holes
into his head, into the darkness.

I ask what woke him?

'A wolf dreamed me' he says.

JACKIE KAY 1961–

BRENDON GALLACHER
For my brother, Maxie

He was seven and I was six, my Brendon Gallacher.
He was Irish and I was Scottish, my Brendon Gallacher.
His father was in prison; he was a cat burglar.
My father was a communist party full-time worker.
He has six brothers and I had one, my Brendon Gallacher.

He would hold my hand and take me by the river
Where we'd talk all about his family being poor.
He'd get his mum out of Glasgow when he got older.
A wee holiday someplace nice. Someplace far.
I'd tell my mum about my Brendon Gallacher

How his mum drank and his daddy was a cat burglar.
And she'd say, 'Why not have him round to dinner?'
No, no, I'd say, he's got big holes in his trousers.
I like meeting him by the burn in the open air.
Then one day after we'd been friends two years,

One day when it was pouring and I was indoors,
My mum says to me, 'I was talking to Mrs Moir
Who lives next door to your Brendon Gallacher
Didn't you say his address was 24 Novar?
She says there are no Gallachers at 24 Novar

There never have been any Gallachers next door.'
And he died then, my Brendon Gallacher,
Flat out on my bedroom floor, his spiky hair,
His impish grin, his funny flapping ear.
Oh Brendon. Oh my Brendon Gallacher.

'. . . The glamour
Of childish days is upon me, my manhood is cast
Down in the flood of remembrance, I weep
* like a child for the past'*

from 'Piano'

WILLIAM SHAKESPEARE 1564–1616

WHEN THAT I WAS AND A LITTLE TINY BOY

When that I was and a little tiny boy,
　With hey, ho, the wind and the rain,
A foolish thing was but a toy,
　For the rain it raineth every day.

But when I came to man's estate,
　With hey, ho, the wind and the rain,
'Gainst knaves and thieves men shut their gate,
　For the rain it raineth every day.

But when I came, alas! to wive,
　With hey, ho, the wind and the rain,
By swaggering could I never thrive,
　For the rain it raineth every day.

But when I came unto my beds,
　With hey, ho, the wind and the rain,
With toss-pots still had drunken heads,
　For the rain it raineth every day.

A great while ago the world begun,
　With hey, ho, the wind and the rain,
But that's all one, our play is done,
　And we'll strive to please you every day.

THOMAS HOOD 1799–1845

I REMEMBER, I REMEMBER

I remember, I remember,
    The house where I was born,
The little window where the sun
    Came peeping in at morn;
He never came a wink too soon,
    Nor brought too long a day,
But now, I often wish the night
    Had borne my breath away.

I remember, I remember,
    The roses, red and white;
The violets, and the lily-cups,
    Those flowers made of light!
The lilacs where the robin built,
    And where my brother set
The laburnum on his birthday –
    The tree is living yet!

I remember, I remember,
    Where I was used to swing;
And thought the air must rush as fresh
    To swallows on the wing:
My spirit flew in feathers then,
    That is so heavy now,
And summer pools could hardly cool
    The fever on my brow!

I remember, I remember,
    The fir trees dark and high;
I used to think their slender tops
    Were close against the sky:
It was a childish ignorance,
    But now 'tis little joy
To know I'm farther off from Heav'n
    Than when I was a boy.

GEORGE ELIOT 1819–80

from BROTHER AND SISTER

I

I cannot choose but think upon the time
When our two lives grew like two buds that kiss
At lightest thrill from the bee's swinging chime,
Because the one so near the other is.

He was the elder and a little man
Of forty inches, bound to show no dread,
And I the girl that puppy-like now ran,
Now lagged behind my brother's larger tread.

I held him wise, and when he talked to me
Of snakes and birds, and which God loved the best,
I thought his knowledge marked the boundary
Where men grew blind, though angels knew the rest.

If he said 'Hush!' I tried to hold my breath;
Wherever he said 'Come!' I stepped in faith.

IX

We had the self-same world enlarged for each
By loving difference of girl and boy:
The fruit that hung on high beyond my reach
He plucked for me, and oft he must employ

A measuring glance to guide my tiny shoe
Where lay firm stepping-stones, or call to mind
'This thing I like my sister may not do,
For she is little, and I must be kind.'

Thus boyish Will the nobler mastery learned
Where inward vision over impulse reigns,
Widening its life with separate life discerned,
A Like unlike, a Self that self restrains.

His years with others must the sweeter be
For those brief days he spent in loving me.

THOMAS HARDY 1846–1928

THE SELF-UNSEEING

Here is the ancient floor,
Footworn and hollowed and thin,
Here was the former door
Where the dead feet walked in.

She sat here in her chair,
Smiling into the fire;
He who played stood there,
Bowing it higher and higher.

Childlike, I danced in a dream;
Blessings emblazoned that day;
Everything glowed with a gleam;
Yet we were looking away!

ROBERT FROST 1874–1963

BIRCHES

When I see birches bend to left and right
Across the lines of straighter darker trees,
I like to think some boy's been swinging them.
But swinging doesn't bend them down to stay
As ice-storms do. Often you must have seen them
Loaded with ice a sunny winter morning
After a rain. They click upon themselves
As the breeze rises, and turn many-coloured
As the stir cracks and crazes their enamel.
Soon the sun's warmth makes them shed crystal shells
Shattering and avalanching on the snow-crust –
Such heaps of broken glass to sweep away
You'd think the inner dome of heaven had fallen.
They are dragged to the withered bracken by the load,
And they seem not to break; though once they are bowed
So low for long, they never right themselves:
You may see their trunks arching in the woods
Years afterwards, trailing their leaves on the ground
Like girls on hands and knees that throw their hair
Before them over their heads to dry in the sun.
But I was going to say when Truth broke in
With all her matter-of-fact about the ice-storm
I should prefer to have some boy bend them
As he went out and in to fetch the cows –
Some boy too far from town to learn baseball,
Whose only play was what he found himself,
Summer or winter, and could play alone.
One by one he subdued his father's trees
By riding them down over and over again
Until he took the stiffness out of them,
And not one but hung limp, not one was left
For him to conquer. He learned all there was
To learn about not launching out too soon
And so not carrying the tree away

Clear to the ground. He always kept his poise
To the top branches, climbing carefully
With the same pains you use to fill a cup
Up to the brim, and even above the brim.
Then he flung outward, feet first, with a swish,
Kicking his way down through the air to the ground.
So was I once myself a swinger of birches.
And so I dream of going back to be.
It's when I'm weary of considerations,
And life is too much like a pathless wood
Where your face burns and tickles with the cobwebs
Broken across it, and one eye is weeping
From a twig's having lashed across it open.
I'd like to get away from earth awhile
And then come back to it and begin over.
May no fate wilfully misunderstand me
And half grant what I wish and snatch me away
Not to return. Earth's the right place for love:
I don't know where it's likely to go better.
I'd like to go by climbing a birch tree,
And climb black branches up a snow-white trunk
Toward heaven, till the tree could bear no more,
But dipped its top and set me down again.
That would be good both going and coming back.
One could do worse than be a swinger of birches.

RAINER MARIA RILKE 1875–1926

FROM A CHILDHOOD

The dark grew ripe like treasure in the room
in which the boy, submerged so deeply, sat.
And as the mother entered like a dream
there trembled, on the silent shelf, a glass.
She sensed it, how the room somehow betrayed her,
and finding, kissed her boy: Are you here? . . .
Slowly his gaze turned hers toward the piano,
for many evenings now she'd played a piece
whose rapture left the child beyond release.

He sat so still. His huge gaze bent
upon her hand which, burdened by the ring,
ploughed as if through snowdrifts deepening
and over the white keys went.

D.H. LAWRENCE 1885–1930

PIANO

Softly, in the dusk, a woman is singing to me:
Taking me back down the vista of years, till I see
A child sitting under the piano, in the boom of the tingling
  strings
And pressing the small, poised feet of a mother who smiles as
  she sings.

In spite of myself, the insidious mastery of song
Betrays me back, till the heart of me weeps to belong
To the old Sunday evenings at home, with winter outside
And hymns in the cosy parlour, the tinkling piano our guide.

So now it is vain for the singer to burst into clamour
With the great black piano appassionato. The glamour
Of childish days is upon me, my manhood is cast
Down in the flood of remembrance, I weep like a child for the past.

T.S. ELIOT 1888–1965

NEW HAMPSHIRE

Children's voices in the orchard
Between the blossom- and the fruit-time:
Golden head, crimson head,
Between the green tip and the root.
Black wing, brown wing, hover over;
Twenty years and the spring is over;
To-day grieves, to-morrow grieves,
Cover me over, light-in-leaves;
Golden head, black wing,
Cling, swing,
Spring, sing,
Swing up into the apple-tree.

LOUIS MACNEICE 1907–63

SOAP SUDS

This brand of soap has the same smell as once in the big
House he visited when he was eight: the walls of the bathroom
  open
To reveal a lawn where a great yellow ball rolls back through
  a hoop
To rest at the head of a mallet held in the hands of a child.

And these were the joys of that house: a tower with a
  telescope;
Two great faded globes, one of the earth, one of the stars;
A stuffed black dog in the hall; a walled garden with bees;
A rabbit warren; a rockery; a vine under glass; the sea.

To which he has now returned. The day of course is fine
And a grown-up voice cries Play! The mallet slowly swings,
Then crack, a great gong booms from the dog-dark hall and
  the ball
Skims forward through the hoop and then through the next
  and then

Through hoops where no hoops were and each dissolves in
  turn
And the grass has grown head-high and an angry voice cries
  Play!
But the ball is lost and the mallet slipped long since from the
  hands
Under the running tap that are not the hands of a child.

KATHLEEN RAINE 1908–

HEIRLOOM

She gave me childhood's flowers,
Heather and wild thyme,
Eyebright and tormentil,
Lichen's mealy cup
Dry on wind-scored stone,
The corbies on the rock,
The rowan by the burn.

Sea-marvels a child beheld
Out in the fisherman's boat,
Fringed pulsing violet
Medusa, sea-gooseberries,
Starfish on the sea-floor,
Cowries and rainbow shells
From pools on a rocky shore.

Gave me her memories,
But kept her last treasure:
'When I was a lass', she said,
'Sitting among the heather,
'Suddenly I saw
'That all the moor was alive!
'I have told no-one before'.

That was my mother's tale.
Seventy years had gone
Since she saw the living skein
Of which the world is woven,
And having seen, knew all;
Through long indifferent years
Treasuring the priceless pearl.

STEPHEN SPENDER 1909–95

MY PARENTS

My parents kept me from children who were rough
Who threw words like stones and wore torn clothes
Their thighs showed through rags they ran in the street
And climbed cliffs and stripped by the country streams.

I feared more than tigers their muscles like iron
Their jerking hands and their knees tight on my arms
I feared the salt coarse pointing of those boys
Who copied my lisp behind me on the road.

They were lithe they sprang out behind hedges
Like dogs to bark at my world. They threw mud
While I looked the other way, pretending to smile.
I longed to forgive them but they never smiled.

ROBERT HAYDEN 1913–80

THOSE WINTER SUNDAYS

Sundays too my father got up early
and put his clothes on in the blueblack cold,
then with cracked hands that ached
from labour in the weekday weather made
banked fires blaze. No one ever thanked him.

I'd wake and hear the cold splintering, breaking.
When the rooms were warm, he'd call,
and slowly I would rise and dress,
fearing the chronic angers of that house,

Speaking indifferently to him,
who had driven out the cold
and polished my good shoes as well.
What did I know, what did I know
of love's austere and lonely offices?

DYLAN THOMAS 1914–53
_____

FERN HILL

Now as I was young and easy under the apple boughs
About the lilting house and happy as the grass was green,
    The night above the dingle starry,
      Time let me hail and climb
    Golden in the heydays of his eyes,
And honoured among wagons I was prince of the apple towns
And once below a time I lordly had the trees and leaves
      Trail with daisies and barley
    Down the rivers of the windfall light.

And as I was green and carefree, famous among the barns
About the happy yard and singing as the farm was home,
    In the sun that is young once only,
      Time let me play and be
    Golden in the mercy of his means,
And green and golden I was huntsman and herdsman, the calves
Sang to my horn, the foxes on the hills barked clear and cold,
      And the sabbath rang slowly
    In the pebbles of the holy streams.

All the sun long it was running, it was lovely, the hay
Fields high as the house, the tunes from the chimneys, it was air
    And playing, lovely and watery
      And fire green as grass.
    And nightly under the simple stars
As I rode to sleep the owls were bearing the farm away,
All the moon long I heard, blessed among stables, the night-jars
    Flying with the ricks and the horses
      Flashing into the dark.

And then to awake, and the farm, like a wanderer white
With the dew, come back, the cock on his shoulder: it was all
    Shining, it was Adam and maiden,
      The sky gathered again

And the sun grew round that very day.
So it must have been after the birth of the simple light
In the first, spinning place, the spellbound horses walking warm
    Out of the whinnying green stable
        On to the fields of praise.

And honoured among foxes and pheasants by the gay house
Under the new made clouds and happy as the heart was long,
    In the sun born over and over,
        I ran my heedless ways,
      My wishes raced through the house high hay
And nothing I cared, at my sky blue trades, that time allows
In all his tuneful turning so few and such morning songs
    Before the children green and golden
        Follow him out of grace,

Nothing I cared, in the lamb white days, that time would take me
Up to the swallow thronged loft by the shadow of my hand,
    In the moon that is always rising,
        Nor that riding to sleep
    I should hear him fly with the high fields
And wake to the farm forever fled from the childless land.
Oh as I was young and easy in the mercy of his means,
        Time held me green and dying
    Though I sang in my chains like the sea.

VERNON SCANNELL 1922–

AFTER THE FIREWORKS

Back into the light and warmth,
Boots clogged with mud, toes
Welded to wedges of cold flesh,
The children warm their hands on mugs
While, on remembered lawns, the flash
Of fireworks dazzles night;
Sparklers spray and rockets swish,
Soar high and break in falling showers
Of glitter; the bonfire gallivants,
Its lavish flames shimmy, prance,
And lick the straddling guy;
We wait for those great leaves of heat
And broken necklaces of light
To dim and die.
And then the children go to bed.
Tomorrow they will search grey ground
For debris of tonight: the sad
And saturated cardboard stems,
The fallen rocket sticks, the charred
Hubs of catherine-wheels;
Then, having gathered all they've found,
They'll leave them scattered carelessly
For us to clear away.
But now the children are asleep,
And you and I sit silently
And hear, from far off in the night,
The last brave rocket burst and fade.
We taste the darkness in the light,
Reflect that fireworks are not cheap
And ask ourselves uneasily
If, even now, we've fully paid.

SEAMUS HEANEY 1939–

FOLLOWER

My father worked with a horse-plough,
His shoulders globed like a full sail strung
Between the shafts and the furrow.
The horses strained at his clicking tongue.

An expert. He would set the wing
And fit the bright steel-pointed sock.
The sod rolled over without breaking.
At the headrig, with a single-pluck

Of reins, the sweating team turned round
And back into the land. His eye
Narrowed and angled at the ground,
Mapping the furrow exactly.

I stumbled in his hob-nailed wake
Fell sometimes on the polished sod;
Sometimes he rode me on his back
Dipping and rising to his plod.

I wanted to grow up and plough,
To close one eye, stiffen my arm,
All I ever did was follow
In his broad shadow round the farm.

I was a nuisance, tripping, falling,
Yapping always. But today
It is my father who keeps stumbling
Behind me, and will not go away.

SEAMUS HEANEY 1939–

THE RAILWAY CHILDREN

When we climbed the slopes of the cutting
We were eye-level with the white cups
Of the telegraph poles and the sizzling wires.

Like lovely freehand they curved for miles
East and miles west beyond us, sagging
Under their burden of swallows.

We were small and thought we knew nothing
Worth knowing. We thought words travelled the wires
In the shiny pouches of raindrops,

Each one seeded full with the light
Of the sky, the gleam of the lines, and ourselves
So infinitesimally scaled

We could stream through the eye of a needle.

BRIAN PATTEN 1946–

WHERE ARE YOU NOW, BATMAN?

Where are you now, Batman? Now that Aunt Heriot has
        reported Robin missing
And Superman's fallen asleep in the sixpenny childhood
        seats?
Where are you now that Captain Marvel's SHAZAM!
        echoes round the auditorium,
The magicians don't hear it,
Must all be deaf . . . or dead . . .
The Purple Monster who came down from the Purple Planet
        disguised as a man
Is wandering aimlessly about the streets
With no way of getting back.
Sir Galahad's been strangled by the Incredible Living Trees,
Zorro killed by his own sword.
Blackhawk has buried the last of his companions
And has now gone off to commit suicide in the disused
        Hangars of Innocence.
The Monster and the Ape still fight it out in a room
Where the walls are continually closing;
Rocketman's fuel tanks gave out over London.
Even Flash Gordon's lost, podgy and helpless
He wanders among the stars
Weeping over the robots he loved
   Half a universe ago.
        My celluloid companions, it's only a few years
Since we first knew you. Yet something in us has already faded.
Has the Terrible Fiend, That Ghastly Adversary,
Mr Old Age, Caught you in his deadly trap,
And come finally to polish you off,
His machinegun dripping with years . . .?

YUSEF KOMUNYAKAA 1947–

SUNDAY AFTERNOONS

They'd latch the screendoors
& pull venetian blinds,

Telling us not to leave the yard.
But we always got lost
Among mayhaw & crabapple.

Juice spilled from our mouths,
& soon we were drunk & brave
As birds diving through saw vines.
Each nest held three or four
Speckled eggs, blue as rage.

Where did we learn to be unkind,
There in the power of holding each egg
While watching dogs in June
Dust & heat, or when we followed
The hawk's slow, deliberate arc?

In the yard, we heard cries
Fused with gospel on the radio,
Loud as shattered glass
In a Saturday-night argument
About trust & money.

We were born between Oh Yeah
& Goddammit. I knew life
Began where I stood in the dark,
Looking out into the light,
& that sometimes I could see

Everything through nothing.
The backyard trees breathed
Like a man running from himself
As my brothers backed away
From the screendoor. I knew

If I held my right hand above my eyes
Like a gambler's visor, I could see
How their bedroom door halved
The dresser mirror like a moon
Held prisoner in the house.

LIZ LOCHHEAD 1948–

REVELATION

I remember once being shown the black bull
when a child at the farm for eggs and milk.
They called him Bob – as though perhaps
you could reduce a monster
with the charm of a friendly name.
At the threshold of his outhouse, someone
held my hand and let me peer inside.
At first, only black
and the hot reek of him. Then he was immense,
his edges merging with the darkness, just
a big bulk and a roar to be really scared of,
a trampling, and a clanking tense with the chain's jerk.
His eyes swivelled in the great wedge of his tossed head.
He roared his rage. His nostrils gaped.

And in the yard outside,
oblivious hens picked their way about.
The faint and rather festive tinkling
behind the mellow stone and hasp was all they knew
of that Black Mass, straining at his chains.
I had always half-known he existed –
this antidote and Anti-Christ his anarchy
threatening the eggs, well rounded, self-contained –
and the placidity of milk.

I ran, my pigtails thumping on my back in fear,
past the big boys in the farm lane
who pulled the wings from butterflies and
blew up frogs with straws.
Past throned hedge and harried nest,
scared of the eggs shattering –
only my small and shaking hand on the jug's rim
in case the milk should spill.

MARY DORCEY 1950–

FIRST LOVE

You were tall and beautiful.
You wore your long brown hair
wound about your head,
your neck stood clear and full
as the stem of a vase.
You held my hand in yours
and we walked slowly, talking
of small familiar happenings
and of the lost secrets of
your childhood. It seems it was

Always autumn then.
The amber trees shook. We laughed
in a wind that cracked the leaves
from black boughs and set them scuffling
about our feet, for me to trample still
and kick in orange clouds
about your face. We would climb dizzy
to the cliff's edge and stare down
at a green and purple sea, the

Wind howling in our ears, as it
tore the breath from white cheeked waves.
You steadied me against
the wheeling screech of gulls, and i
loved to think that but for your strength
i would tumble to the rocks below
to the fated death, your stories made me
dream of. I don't remember
that i looked in your eyes or that we
ever asked an open question. Our thoughts

Passed through our blood, it seemed,
and the slightest pressure of our hands
decided all issues wordlessly.

We watched in silence by the shore
the cold spray against our skin,
in mutual need of the water's fierce,
inhuman company, that gave promise
of some future, timeless refuge from
all the fixed anxieties of our world.
As we made for home

We faced into the wind, my thighs
were grazed by its icy teeth, you
gathered your coat about me and i
hurried our steps towards home, fire
and the comfort of your sweet, strong tea.
We moved bound in step.
You sang me songs of Ireland's sorrows
and of proud women, loved and lost.
I knew then, they set for me
a brilliant stage of characters, who

Even now, can seem more real
than my most intimate friends.
We walked together, hand in hand.
You were tall and beautiful,
you wore your long brown hair wound
about your head, your neck stood
clear and full as the stem of a vase.
I was young – you were my mother
and it seems, it was always
autumn then.

'It is not now as it hath been of yore –
Turn whereso'er I may, . . .
The things which I have seen I now can
see no more'

from 'Ode'

ANDREW MARVEL 1621–78

THE PICTURE OF LITTLE T.C. IN A PROSPECT OF FLOWERS

I

See with what simplicity
This nymph begins her golden days!
In the green grass she loves to lie,
And there with her fair aspect tames
The wilder flowers, and gives them names:
But only with the roses plays;
         And them does tell
What colour best becomes them, and what smell.

II

Who can foretell for what high cause
This darling of the gods was born!
Yet this is she whose chaster laws
The wanton Love shall one day fear,
And, under her command severe,
See his brow broke and ensigns torn.
         Happy, who can
Appease this virtuous enemy of man!

III

O, then let me in time compound,
And parley with those conquering eyes;
Ere they have tried their force to wound,
Ere, with their glancing wheels, they drive
In triumph over hearts that strive,
And them that yield but more despise.
         Let me be laid,
Where I may see thy glories from some shade.

IV

Meantime, whilst every verdant thing
Itself does at thy beauty charm,
Reform the errors of the spring;
Make that the tulips may have share
Of sweetness, seeing they are fair;
And roses of their thorns disarm:
            But most procure
That violets may a longer age endure.

V

But, O young beauty of the woods,
Whom Nature courts with fruits and flowers,
Gather the flowers, but spare the buds;
Lest Flora angry at thy crime,
To kill her infants in their prime,
Do quickly make the example yours;
            And, ere we see,
Nip in the blossom all our hopes and thee.

WILLIAM WORDSWORTH 1770–1850

from ODE
Intimations of Immortality from Recollections of Early Childhood

The Child is father of the Man;
And I could wish my days to be
Bound each to each by natural piety.

I

There was a time when meadow, grove, and stream,
The earth, and every common sight,
        To me did seem
        Apparelled in celestial light,
The glory and the freshness of a dream:
It is not now as it hath been of yore –
        Turn whereso'er I may,
        By night or day,
The things which I have seen I now can see no more.

V

Our birth is but a sleep and a forgetting:
The Soul that rises with us, our life's Star,
        Hath had elsewhere its setting,
            And cometh from afar:
        Not in entire forgetfulness,
        And not in utter nakedness,
But trailing clouds of glory do we come
        From God, who is our home:
Heaven lies about us in our infancy!
Shades of the prison-house begin to close
        Upon the growing Boy
            But he
Beholds the light, and whence it flows,
        He sees it in his joy;
The Youth, who daily farther from the east
        Must travel, still is Nature's Priest,
        And by the vision splendid

Is on his way attended;
At length the Man perceives it die away,
And fade into the light of common day.

VI

Earth fills her lap with pleasures of her own;
Yearnings she hath in her own natural kind,
And, even with something of a Mother's mind,
    And no unworthy aim,
    The homely Nurse doth all she can
To make her foster child, her Inmate Man,
    Forget the glories he hath known,
And that imperial palace whence he came.

VII

Behold the Child among his newborn blisses,
A six-years' Darling of a pygmy size!
See, where mid work of his own hand he lies,
Fretted by sallies of his mother's kisses,
With light upon him from his father's eyes!
See, at his feet, some little plan or chart,
Some fragment from his dream of human life,
Shaped by himself with newly-learnèd art;
    A wedding or a festival,
    A mourning or a funeral;
      And this hath now his heart,
    And unto this he frames his song;
      Then will he fit his tongue
To dialogues of business, love, or strife;
    But it will not be long
    Ere this be thrown aside,
    And with new joy and pride
The little Actor cons another part;
Filling from time to time his 'humorous stage'

With all the Persons, down to palsied Age,
That Life brings with her in her equipage;
  As if his whole vocation
  Were endless imitation.

VIII

Thou, whose exterior semblance doth belie
  Thy Soul's immensity;
Thou best Philosopher, who yet dost keep
Thy heritage, thou Eye among the blind,
That, deaf and silent, read'st the eternal deep,
Haunted forever by the eternal mind –
  Mighty Prophet! Seer blest!
  On whom those truths do rest,
Which we are toiling all our lives to find,
In darkness lost, the darkness of the grave;
Thou, over whom thy Immortality
Broods like the Day, a Master o'er a Slave,
A Presence which is not to be put by;
Thou little child, yet glorious in the might
Of heaven-born freedom on thy being's height,
Why with such earnest pains dost thou provoke
The years to bring the inevitable yoke,
Thus blindly with thy blessedness at strife?
Full soon thy Soul shall have her earthly freight,
And custom lie upon thee with a weight,
Heavy as frost, and deep almost as life!

IX

  O joy! that in our embers
  Is something that doth live,
  That nature yet remembers
  What was so fugitive!
The thought of our past years in me doth breed

Perpetual benediction: not indeed
For that which is most worthy to be blest;
Delight and liberty, the simple creed
Of Childhood, whether busy or at rest,
With new-fledged hope still fluttering in his breast –
    Not for these I raise
      The song of thanks and praise;
       But for those obstinate questionings
       Of sense and outward things,
       Fallings from us, vanishings;
       Blank misgivings of a Creature
Moving about in worlds not realised,
High instincts before which our mortal Nature
Did tremble like a guilty Thing surprised:
      But for those first affections,
      Those shadowy recollections,
    Which, be they what they may,
Are yet the fountain light of all our day,
Are yet a master light of all our seeing;
    Uphold us, cherish, and have power to make
Our noisy years seem moments in the being
Of the eternal Silence: truths that wake,
      To perish never;
Which neither listlessness, nor mad endeavour,
      Nor Man nor Boy,
Nor all that is at enmity with joy,
Can utterly abolish or destroy!
    Hence in a season of calm weather
    Though inland far we be,
Our Souls have sight of that immortal sea
    Which brought us hither,
    Can in a moment travel thither,
And see the Children sport upon the shore,
And hear the mighty waters rolling evermore.

WILLIAM WORDSWORTH 1770–1850

from THE PRELUDE

There was a Boy; ye knew him well, ye cliffs
And islands of Winander! — many a time,
At evening, when the earliest stars began
To move along the edges of the hills,
Rising or setting, would he stand alone,
Beneath the trees, or by the glimmering lake;
And there, with fingers interwoven, both hands
Pressed closely palm to palm and to his mouth
Uplifted, he, as through an instrument,
Blew mimic hootings to the silent owls,
That they might answer him. — And they would shout
Across the watery vale, and shout again,
Responsive to his call, — with quivering peals,
And long halloos, and screams, and echoes loud
Redoubled and redoubled; concourse wild
Of jocund din! And, when there came a pause
Of silence such as baffled his best skill:
Then, sometimes, in that silence, while he hung
Listening, a gentle shock of mild surprise
Has carried far into his heart the voice
Of mountain-torrents; or the visible scene
Would enter unawares into his mind
With all its solemn imagery, its rocks,
Its woods, and that uncertain heaven received
Into the bosom of the steady lake.

CHARLES LAMB 1775–1834

THE OLD FAMILIAR FACES

I have had playmates, I have had companions,
In my days of childhood, in my joyful school-days,
All, all are gone, the old familiar faces.

I have been laughing, I have been carousing,
Drinking late, sitting late, with my bosom cronies,
All, all are gone, the old familiar faces.

I loved a love once, fairest among women:
Closed are her doors on me, I must not see her –
All, all are gone, the old familiar faces.

I have a friend, a kinder friend has no man;
Like an ingrate, I felt my friend abruptly;
Left him, to muse on the old familiar faces.

Ghost-like I paced round the haunts of my childhood,
Earth seemed a desert I was bound to traverse,
Seeking to find the old familiar faces.

Friend of my bosom, thou more than a brother,
Why wert not thou born in my father's dwelling?
So might we talk of the old familiar faces –

How some they have died, and some they have left me,
And some are taken from me; all are departed;
All, all are gone, the old familiar faces.

WALT WHITMAN 1819–92

THERE WAS A CHILD WENT FORTH

There was a child went forth every day,
And the first object he look'd upon, that object he became,
And that object became part of him for the day or a certain part of
   the day,
Or for many years or stretching cycles of years.

The early lilacs became part of this child,
And grass and white and red morning-glories, and white and red
   clover, and the song of the phœbe-bird,
And the Third-month lambs and the sow's pink-faint litter, and the
   mare's foal and the cow's calf,
And the noisy brood of the barnyard or by the mire of the
   pondside,
And the fish suspending themselves so curiously below there, and
   the beautiful curious liquid,
And the water-plants with their graceful flat heads, all became part
   of him.

The field-sprouts of Fourth-month and Fifth-month became part
   of him,
Winter-grain sprouts and those of the light-yellow corn, and the
   esculent roots of the garden,
And the apple-trees cover'd with blossoms and the fruit afterward,
   and wood-berries, and the commonest weeds by the road,
And the old drunkard staggering home from the outhouse of the
   tavern whence he had lately risen,
And the schoolmistress that pass'd on her way to the school,
And the friendly boys that pass'd, and the quarrelsome boys,
And the tidy and fresh-cheek'd girls, and the barefoot negro boy
   and girl,
And all the changes of city and country wherever he went.

His own parents, he that had father'd him and she that had
   conceiv'd him in her womb and birth'd him,

They gave this child more of themselves than that,
They gave him afterward every day, they became part of him.
The mother at home quietly placing the dishes on the supper-table,
The mother with mild words, clean her cap and gown, a wholesome
    odour falling off her person and clothes as she walks by,
The father, strong, self-sufficient, manly, mean, anger'd, unjust,
The blow, the quick loud word, the tight bargain, the crafty lure,
The family usages, the language, the company, the furniture, the
    yearning and swelling heart,
Affection that will not be gainsay'd, the sense of what is real, the
    thought if after all it should prove unreal,
The doubts of day-time and the doubts of night-time, the curious
    whether and how,
Whether that which appears so is so, or is it all flashes and specks?
Men and women crowding fast in the streets, if they are not flashes
    and specks what are they?
The streets themselves and the façades of houses, and goods in the
    windows,
Vehicles, teams, the heavy-plank'd wharves, the huge crossing at
    the ferries,
The village on the highland seen from afar at sunset, the river
    between,
Shadows, aureola and mist, the light falling on roofs and gables
    of white or brown two miles off,
The schooner near by sleepily dropping down the tide, the little
    boat slack-tow'd astern,
The hurrying tumbling waves, quick-broken crests, slapping,
The strata of colour'd clouds, the long bar of maroon-tint away
    solitary by itself, the spread of purity it lies motionless in,
The horizon's edge, the flying sea-crow, the fragrance of salt
    marsh and shore mud,
These became part of that child who went forth every day, and who
    now goes, and will always go forth every day.

THOMAS HARDY 1840–1928

THE CHILDREN AND SIR NAMELESS

Sir Nameless, once of Athelhall, declared:
'These wretched children romping in my park
Trample the herbage till the soil is bared,
And yap and yell from early morn till dark!
Go keep them harnessed to their set routines:
Thank God I've none to hasten my decay;
For green remembrance there are better means
Than offspring, who but wish their sires away.'

Sir Nameless of that mansion said anon:
'To be perpetuate for my mightiness
Sculpture must image me when I am gone.'
 – He forthwith summoned carvers there express
To shape a figure stretching seven-odd feet
(For he was tall) in alabaster stone,
With shield, and crest, and casque, and sword complete:
When done a statelier work was never known.

Three hundred years hied; Church-restorers came,
And, no one of his lineage being traced,
They thought an effigy so large in frame
Best fitted for the floor. There it was placed,
Under the seats for schoolchildren. And they
Kicked out his name, and hobnailed off his nose;
And, as they yawn through sermon-time, they say,
'Who was this old stone man beneath our toes?'

GERARD MANLEY HOPKINS 1844–89

SPRING AND FALL:
to a young child

Margaret, are you gríeving
Over Goldengrove unleaving?
Leáves, líke the things of man, you
With your fresh thoughts care for, can you?
Áh! ás the heart grows older
It will come to such sights colder
By and by, nor spare a sigh
Though worlds of wanwood leafmeal lie;
And yet you wíll weep and know why
Now no matter, child, the name:
Sórrow's spríngs áre the same.
Nor mouth had, no nor mind, expressed
What heart heard of, ghost guessed:
It ís the blight man was born for,
It is Margaret you mourn for.

C. DAY LEWIS 1904–72

PASSAGE FROM CHILDHOOD

His earliest memory, the mood
Fingered and frail as maidenhair,
Was this – a china cup somewhere
In a green, deep wood.
He lives to find again somewhere
That wood, that homely cup; to taste all
Its chill, imagined dews; to dare
The dangerous crystal.

Who can say what misfeatured elf
First led him into that lifelong
Passage of mirrors where, so young,
He saw himself
Balanced as Blondin, more headstrong
Than baby Hercules, rare as a one-
Cent British Guiana, above the wrong
And common run?

He knew the secrecy of squirrels,
The foolish doves' antiphony,
And what wrens fear. He was gun-shy,
Hating all quarrels.
Life was a hostile land to spy,
Full of questions he dared not ask
Lest the answer in mockery
Or worse unmask.

Quick to injustice, quick he grew
This hermit and contorted shell.
Self-pity like a thin rain fell,
Fouling the view:
Then tree-trunks seemed wet roots of hell,
Wren or catkin might turn vicious,
The dandelion clock could tell
Nothing auspicious.

No exile has ever looked so glum
With the pines fretful overhead,
Yet he felt at home in the gothic glade –
More than at home.
You will forgive him that he played
Bumble-puppy on the small mossed lawn
All by himself for hours, afraid
Of being born.

Lying awake one night, he saw
Eternity stretched like a howl of pain:
He was tiny and terrible, a new pin
On a glacier's floor.
Very few they are who have lain
With eternity and lived to tell it:
There's a secret process in his brain
And he cannot sell it.

Now, beyond reach of sense or reason,
His life walks in a glacial sleep
For ever, since he drank that cup
And found it poison.
He's one more ghost, engaged to keep
Eternity's long hours and mewed
Up in live flesh with no escape
From solitude.

STEPHEN SPENDER 1909–95

BOY, CAT, CANARY

Our whistling son called his canary Hector.
'Why?' I asked. 'Because I had always about me
More of Hector with his glittering helmet than
Achilles with his triple-thewed shield.' He let Hector
Out of his cage, fly up to the ceiling, perch on his chair, hop
On to his table where the sword lay bright among books
While he sat in his yellow jersey, doing his homework.
Once, hearing a shout, I entered his room, saw what carnage:
The Siamese cat had worked his tigerish scene;
Hector lay on the floor of his door-open cage
Wings still fluttering, flattened against the sand.
Parallel, horizontal, on the rug, the boy lay
Mouth biting against it, fists hammering boards.
'Tomorrow let him forget.' I prayed, 'Let him not see
What I see in this room of miniature Iliad –
The golden whistling howled down by the dark.'

C.H. SISSON 1914–

ELLICK FARM

The larks flew up like jack-in-the-boxes
From my moors, and the fields were edged with foxgloves.

The farm lay neatly within the hollow
The gables climbing, the barn beside the doorway.

If I had climbed into the loft I should have found a boy
Forty years back, among the bales of hay.

He would have known certainly all that I know
Seeing it in the muck-strewn cobbles below.

(Under the dark rim of the near wood
The tears gathered as under an eyelid.)

It would have surprised him to see a tall man
Who had travelled far, pretending to be him.

But that he should have been turning verses, half dumb
After half a lifetime, would least have surprised him.

PHILIP LARKIN 1922–85

COMING

On longer evenings,
Light, chill and yellow,
Bathes the serene
Foreheads of houses.
A thrush sings,
Laurel-surrounded
In the deep bare garden,
Its fresh-peeled voice
Astonishing the brickwork.
It will be spring soon,
It will be spring soon –
And I, whose childhood
Is a forgotten boredom,
Feel like a child
Who comes on a scene
Of adult reconciling,
And can understand nothing
But the unusual laughter,
And starts to be happy.

PHILIP LARKIN 1922–85

TAKE ONE HOME FOR THE KIDDIES

On shallow straw, in shadeless glass,
Huddled by empty bowls, they sleep:
No dark, no dam, no earth, no grass –
Mam, get us one of them to keep.

Living toys are something novel,
But it soon wears off somehow.
Fetch the shoebox, fetch the shovel –
Mam, we're playing funerals now.

13 August 1960

PHILIP LARKIN 1922–85

THIS BE THE VERSE

They fuck you up, your mum and dad.
    They may not mean to, but they do.
They fill you with the faults they had
    And add some extra, just for you.

But they were fucked up in their turn
    By fools in old-style hats and coats,
Who half the time were soppy-stern
    And half at one another's throats.

Man hands on misery to man.
    It deepens like a coastal shelf.
Get out as early as you can,
    And don't have any kids yourself.

ELIZABETH JENNINGS 1926–

A CHILD IN THE NIGHT

The child stares at the stars. He does not know
Their names. He does not care. Time halts for him
And he is standing on the earth's far rim
As all the sky surrenders its bright show.

He will not feel like this again until
He falls in love. He will not be possessed
By dispossession till he has caressed
A face and in its eyes seen stars stand still.

ELIZABETH JENNINGS 1926–

SONG AT THE BEGINNING OF AUTUMN

Now watch this autumn that arrives
In smells. All looks like summer still;
Colours are quite unchanged, the air
On green and white serenely thrives.
Heavy the trees with growth and full
The fields. Flowers flourish everywhere.

Proust who collected time within
A child's cake would understand
The ambiguity of this –
Summer still raging while a thin
Column of smoke stirs from the land
Proving that autumn gropes for us.

But every season is a kind
Of rich nostalgia. We give names –
Autumn and summer, winter, spring –
As though to unfasten from the mind
Our moods and give them outward forms.
We want the certain, solid thing.

But I am carried back against
My will into a childhood where
Autumn is bonfires, marbles, smoke;
I lean against my window fenced
From evocations in the air.
When I said autumn, autumn broke.

DEREK WALCOTT 1930–

A LESSON FOR THIS SUNDAY

The growing idleness of summer grass
With its frail kites of furious butterflies
Requests the lemonade of simple praise
In scansion gentler than my hammock swings
And rituals no more upsetting than a
Black maid shaking linen as she sings
The plain notes of some protestant hosanna
Since I lie idling from the thought in things.

Or so they should. Until I hear the cries
Of two small children hunting yellow wings,
Who break my sabbath with the thought of sin.
Brother and sister, with a common pin,
frowning like serious lepidopterists.
The little surgeon pierces the thin eyes.
Crouched on plump haunches, as a mantis prays
She shrieks to eviscerate its abdomen.
The lesson is the same. The maid removes
Both prodigies from their interest in science.
The girl, in lemon frock, begins to scream
As the maimed, teetering thing attempts its flight.
She is herself a thing of summery light,
Frail as a flower in this blue August air,
Not marked for some late grief that cannot speak.

The mind swings inward on itself in fear
Swayed towards nausea from each normal sign.
Heredity of cruelty everywhere,
And everywhere the frocks of summer torn,
The long look back to see where choice is born,
As summer grass sways to the scythe's design.

FLEUR ADCOCK 1934–

FOR ANDREW

'Will I die?' you ask. And so I enter on
The dutiful exposition of that which you
Would rather not know, and I rather not tell you.
To soften my 'Yes' I offer compensations –
Age and fulfilment 'It's so far away;
You will have children and grandchildren by then')
And indifference ('By then you will not care').
No need: you cannot believe me, convinced
That if you always eat plenty of vegetables
And are careful crossing the street you will live for ever.
And so we close the subject, with much unsaid –
This, for instance: Though you and I may die
Tomorrow or next year, and nothing remain
Of our stock, of the unique, preciously-hoarded
Inimitable genes we carry in us,
It is possible that for many generations
There will exist, sprung from whatever seeds,
Children straight-limbed, with clear enquiring voices,
Bright-eyed as you. Or so I like to think:
Sharing in this your childish optimism.

SEAMUS HEANEY 1939–

A KITE FOR MICHAEL AND CHRISTOPHER

All through that Sunday afternoon
a kite flew above Sunday,
a tightened drumhead, an armful of blown chaff.

I'd seen it grey and slippy in the making,
I'd tapped it when it dried out white and stiff,
I'd tied the bows of newspaper
along its six-foot tail.

But now it was far up like a small black lark
and now it dragged as if the bellied string
were a wet rope hauled upon
to lift a shoal.

My friend says that the human soul
is about the weight of a snipe
yet the soul at anchor there,
the string that sags and ascends,
weighs like a furrow assumed into the heavens.

Before the kite plunges down into the wood
and this line goes useless
take in your two hands, boys, and feel
the strumming, rooted, long-tailed pull of grief.
You were born fit for it.
Stand in here in front of me
and take the strain.

DOUGLAS DUNN 1942–

WHITE FIELDS

An aeroplane, its red and green night-lights
Spotting its distant noise in the darkness;
'Jack Frost', you say, pointing to white fields
Sparkling. My eyes accept the dark, the fields
Extend, spreading and drifting, fences rising
Before the black hedge that zips beside the road
I'm told I must never try to cross without you.
'What time is it?' – 'The middle of the night!
You've had a dream, I heard you shout.'
It woke me and I cried aloud, until
My mother came and showed me the farm
Wasn't burning, the school still had its roof,
There was no one hidden in the little fir trees.
'Only an aeroplane!' As if you meant by that
That there in 1948 in Renfrewshire
We were safe from fear, and the white eyes
Of dead Jews were just photographs
In a terrible past, a neighbour's magazine.
'Only an aeroplane!' Unsleeping factories,
All night you busied overhead, and flames
Flushed out my cities made of shoe-boxes
And dominoes, my native village of shaws.
So innocent machine! I had a toy like you
That I made buzz and drone like Leaper's bees,
From which I dropped the A-bomb on John's pram,
Crumpling the hand-embroidered sheets.
    Our breath melted ice on the window-pane.
Fields drizzled on the glass, opening strips
Of short-lived clarity, and fingernails of ice
Slid to the sill. 'No harm will come to us.'
I slept. Till now I've slept, dreaming of mice
Burrowing under the crusted tufts of snow
That heaviest fall had left us with,
Our planet flooded into continents

Of stray, white islands, a sea too cold to swim.
Till now I've slept, and waking, I reject
Your generation, an old copy of *Everybody's*
Thrown out with *Film Fun* and the tea leaves,
Bulldozed by a conscript from our village
Into a pit dug by forced labour.
So easily is love shed, I hardly feel it.
   White fields, your angled frost filed sharply
Bright over undisturbed grasses, do not soothe
As similes of innocence or idle deaths
That must happen anyway, an unmoral blankness;
Be unforgiving stillness, natural, what is:
Crimes uttered in landscape, smoke-darkened snow.
   Trains in my distance altered. Cattle trucks
Seemed to chug through Georgetown, a station
Where a fat man in a black uniform kept hens
On the platform. The waggons sprouted arms
And dropped dun, and no one sang
'Ten Green Bottles' or 'The Sash.' Offensive outings.

Six years old! And I lived through the worst of it!

JANE SHORE 1947–

HIGH HOLY DAYS

It was hot. A size too large,
my wool winter suit scratched.
Indian summer flaring up through fall.
The shul's broken window
bled sunlight on the congregation; the Red Sea
of the scarlet carpet parted the women from the men.
Mother next to daughter, father next to son
flipped through prayerbooks in unison
trying to keep the place. Across the aisle,
my father wore a borrowed prayershawl.
A black yarmulke covered his bald spot.

The rabbi unlocked the ark
and slid the curtain open. Propped inside,
two scrolls of the Torah dressed like matching dolls,
each, a king and a queen. Ribbons hung down
from their alabaster satin jackets;
each one wore two silver crowns.
I wondered, could the ancient kings
have been so small? So small,
and still have vanquished our enemies?

The cantor's voice rose
like smoke over a sacrificial altar,
and lambs, we rose to echo the refrain.
Each time we sat down
my mother rearranged her skirt.
Each time we stood up
my head hurt from the heat, dizzy
from tripping over the alphabet's
black spikes and lyres,
stick-figure batallions marching to defend
the Second Temple of Jerusalem.

Rocking on their heels, boats
anchored in the harbour of devotion,
the temple elders davenned Kaddish, mourning the dead.
Our neighbour who owned the laundry down the street
covered his left wrist out of habit –
numbers indelible as those
he inked on my father's shirt collars.
Once, I saw that whole arm disappear
into a tub of soapy shirts,

rainbowed, buoyant as the pastel clouds
in *The Illustrated Children's Bible*,
where God's enormous hand reached down
and stopped a heathen army in its tracks.
But on the white-hot desert of the page
I was reading, it was noon,
the marching letters swam, the regiments
wavered in the heat,
a red rain falling on their ranks.
I watched it fall one drop at a time.
I felt faint. And breathed out sharply,
my nose spattering blood across the page.

I watched it fall, and thought,
you are a Chosen One,
the child to lead your tribe.
I looked around the swaying room.
Why would God choose me
to lead this congregation of mostly strangers,
defend them against the broken windows,
the spray-painted writing on the walls?

Overhead, the red bulb of the everlasting light
was burning. As if God held me in His fist,

I stumbled down the synagogue stairs
just in time to hear
a cyclone of breath twist through
the shofar, a battle cry so powerful
it blasted city walls to rubble.
And I reeled home through the dazed traffic
of the business day –
past shoppers, past my school,
in session as usual,
spat like Jonah from the whale
back into the Jew-hating world.

ACKNOWLEDGEMENTS

— ◇ —

The publishers would like to acknowledge the following for permission to reproduce copyright material. Every effort has been made to trace copyright holders but in a few cases this has proved impossible. The publishers would be interested to hear from any copyright holders not here acknowledged.

26. A.P. Watt Ltd on behalf of Michael Yeats for 'A Prayer for my Daughter' from *The Collected Poems of W.B. Yeats*.

30, 77, 132. 'Prayer Before Birth', 'Autobiography' and 'Soap Suds' from *Collected Poems* by Louis MacNeice. Reproduced by permission of David Higham Associates.

31. Carcanet Press for 'Child Waking' from *Collected Poems* (1988) by E.J. Scovell.

32, 45, 134, 163. Faber and Faber Ltd for 'To My Daughter', 'An Elementary School Classroom in a Slum', 'My Parents' and 'Boy, Cat, Canary' from *Collected Poems* by Stephen Spender.

33. J.M. Dent for 'The Unborn Daughter' from *Collected Poems 1945–1990* by R.S. Thomas, published by J.M. Dent & Sons.

34. Extract from *Under Milk Wood* by Dylan Thomas, published by J.M. Dent. Reprinted by permission of David Higham Associates.

35, 165. Born Yesterday' and 'Coming' are reprinted from *The Less Deceived* by Philip Larkin by permission of The Marvell Press, England and Australia.

36. Faber and Faber Ltd for 'Full Moon and Little Frieda' from *Wodwo* by Ted Hughes.

37, 38. Faber and Faber Ltd for 'Morning Song' and 'You're' from *Collected Poems* by Sylvia Plath.

39. Robson Books for 'And Some of the Larger Pieces That You See are Called Uncles' from *Teaching the Wind Plurals* by Nigel Forde.

44, 161. 'Walking Away' and 'Passage From Childhood' from *The Complete Poems* by C. Day Lewis, published by Sinclair-Stevenson (1992), copyright © 1992 in this edition and the estate of C Day Lewis.

46. 'Timothy Winters' from *Collected Poems* by Charles Causley, published by Macmillan. Reproduced by permission of David Higham Associates.

47. 'September, The First Day of School' from *The Collected Poems of Howard Nemerov*. Reproduced with the permission of Mrs Howard Nemerov.

49, 166, 167. Faber and Faber Ltd for 'The School in August', 'Take One Home for the Kiddies' and 'This Be the Verse' from *Collected Poems* by Philip Larkin.

50, Faber and Faber Ltd for 'Deaf School' from *Moortown* by Ted Hughes.

– Acknowledgements –

51. 'The Lesson' from *A Tropical Childhood and Other Poems* by Edward Lucie-Smith, published by Oxford University Press. Copyright © the author 1961. Reproduced by permission of the author c/o Rogers, Coleridge and White, 20 Powis Mews, London W11 1JN.

52. 'For Heidi with Blue Hair'. © Fleur Adcock 1983. Reprinted from *The Incident Book* by Fleur Adcock (1986) by permission of Oxford University Press.

53. 'First Day at School' by Roger McGough. Reprinted by permission of The Peters Fraser and Dunlop Group Ltd on behalf of Roger McGough. © Roger McGough.

54. 'Gust Becos I Cud Not Spel' from *Gargling with Jelly* by Brian Patten (Viking, 1985). Copyright © the author 1985. Reproduced by permission of the author c/o Rogers, Coleridge and White, 20 Powis Mews, London W11 1JN.

55, 66. 'The School Hamster's Holiday' and 'Attention Seeking' from *Three Has Gone*. Published by permission of the author.

60. 'Matilda' from *Complete Verse* by Hilaire Belloc, published by Random House UK Ltd. Reprinted by permission of The Peters Fraser and Dunlop Group Ltd on behalf of: *The Estate of Hilaire Belloc.* © Estate of Hilaire Belloc.

62. 'The Lion and Albert'. Words by George Marriott Edgar. Copyright 1933 Francis, Day and Hunter Ltd, London WC2H 0EA. Reproduced by permission of International Music Publications Ltd.

65. Little Johnny's Confession' from *Grinning Jack* by Brian Patten, first published by Unwin Paperbacks, 1990. Copyright © the author 1990. Reproduced by permission of the author c/o Rogers, Coleridge and White, 20 Powis Mews, London W11 1JN.

76. 'Bombing Casualties' is from *Selected Poetry* by Herbert Read, published by Sinclair Stevenson. Reproduced by permission of David Higham Associates.

78, 98. 'Squatter's Children' and 'Sestina' are from *The Complete Poems 1927–1979* by Elizabeth Bishop. Copyright 1979, 1983 by Alice Helen Methfessel. Reprinted with the permission of Farrar, Straus & Giroux, Inc.

79. 'Death of a Son' from *Selected Poems* by Jon Silkin, published by Sinclair-Stevenson.

81, 139, 140, 172. Faber and Faber Ltd for 'Mid-Term Break', 'Follower', 'The Railway Children' and 'A Kite for Michael and Christopher' from *Opened Ground* by Seamus Heaney.

82. Faber and Faber Ltd for 'Tich Miller' from *Making Cocoa for Kingsley Amis* by Wendy Cope.

92. 'The Little Dancers' by Laurence Binyon is reprinted by permission of The Society of Authors, on behalf of the Laurence Binyon Estate.

93. Egmont Children's Books for 'Buckingham Palace' from *When We Were Very Young* by A.A. Milne published by Methuen Children's Books.

94. Faber and Faber Ltd for 'Childhood' from *Collected Poems* by Edwin Muir.

95. John Murray for 'Hunter Trials' from *Collected Poems* by John Betjeman.

96. 'You Grow Like a Beanstalk' is from *Poems* by Seán Rafferty, published by Etruscan Books (1999), edited by Nicholas Johnson.

100. 'Frozen Canal' is from *An Attitude of Mind* by John Cassidy. Reproduced by permission of the author.

101. Faber and Faber Ltd for 'Chocs' from *Meeting Midnight* by Carol Ann Duffy.

102. 'Going to See *King Lear*' from *Other Lovers* by Jackie Kay, published by Bloodaxe Books.

113. The Literary Trustees of Walter de la Mare and The Society of Authors as their representative for 'The Children of Stare'.

116. 'The Primer' from *The Shade Seller: New and Selected Poems* by Josephine Jacobsen (Doubleday, New York, 1974. Reproduced with the permission of the author.

117. 'A Sick Child' is from *The Complete Poems* by Randall Jarell. Copyright © 1969 by Mrs Randall Jarrell. Reprinted with the permission of Farrar, Straus & Giroux Inc. and Faber and Faber.

118. 'A Child Half-Asleep' is from *Tony Connor: New and Selected Poems*, published by Anvil Press Poetry (1982).

119. 'Brendon Gallacher' from *Two's Company* by Jackie Kay (Blackie 1992). Copyright © Jackie Kay 1992. Reproduced by permission of Penguin Books Ltd.

127. The Estate of Robert Frost for 'Birches' from *The Poetry of Robert Frost* edited by Edward Connery Lathem, published by Jonathan Cape.

130. Laurence Pollinger Ltd and the Estate of Frieda Lawrence Ravagli for 'Piano' from *The Complete Poems of D.H. Lawrence*.

131. Faber and Faber Ltd for 'New Hampshire' from *Collected Poems* by T.S. Eliot.

133. 'Heirloom' from *The Lost Country* by Kathleen Raine. Reprinted by permission of the author.

135. 'Those Winter Sundays', copyright © 1966 by Robert Hayden, from *Collected Poems of Robert Hayden* by Frederick Glaysher, editor. Reprinted by permission of Liveright Publishing Corporation.

136. 'Fern Hill' from *Collected Poems* by Dylan Thomas, published by J.M. Dent. Reproduced by permission of David Higham Associates.

138. Robson Books for 'After the Fireworks' from *Collected Poems 1950–93* by Vernon Scannell.

141. 'Where Are You Now, Batman?' from *Grinning Jack* by Brian Patten, first published by Unwin Paperbacks, 1990. Copyright © the author 1990. Reproduced by permission of the author c/o Rogers, Coleridge and White, 20 Powis Mews, London W11 1JN.

142. 'Sunday Afternoons' is from *Magic City* (Middletown, Conn: Wesleyan University

Press, 1992). Copyright 1992 by Yusef Komunyakaa. Reprinted with the permission of the University Press of New England.

144. Polygon for 'Revelation' from *Revelation* by Liz Lochhead.

145. 'First Love' is from *Bread and Roses*, the anthology of nineteenth and twentieth century poetry by women, published by Virago Press (1982, 1986, 1989).

164. Carcanet Press Ltd. for 'Ellick Farm' from *Collected Poems* (1984) by C.H. Sisson.

168, 169. 'A Child in the Night' and 'Song at the Beginning of Autumn' from *Collected Poems* by Elizabeth Jennings, published by Carcanet. Reproduced by permission of David Higham Associates.

170. 'A Lesson for This Sunday' is from *In a Green Night* by Derek Walcott. Reprinted with the permission of Farrar, Straus & Giroux, Inc.

171. 'For Andrew' © copyright Fleur Adcock 1983. Reprinted from *Selected Poems* by Fleur Adcock (1983) by permission of Oxford University Press.

173. Faber and Faber Ltd for 'White Fields' from *Selected Poems* by Douglas Dunn.

175. The University of Massachusetts Press for 'High Holy Days' from *The Minute Hand* by Jane Shore, published by the University of Massachusetts (Amherst, 1987), copyright © Jane Shore 1987.

INDEX OF POETS' NAMES

— ◇ —

INDEX OF FIRST LINES

— ◇ —

Also available from BBC Worldwide:

THE NATION'S FAVOURITE POEMS
ISBN: 0 563 38782 3

THE NATION'S FAVOURITE POEMS
(hardback gift edition)
ISBN: 0 563 38487 5

THE NATION'S FAVOURITE LOVE POEMS
ISBN: 0 563 38378 X

THE NATION'S FAVOURITE LOVE POEMS
(hardback gift edition)
ISBN: 0 563 38432 8

THE NATION'S FAVOURITE COMIC POEMS
ISBN: 0 563 38451 4

THE NATION'S FAVOURITE TWENTIETH CENTURY
POEMS
ISBN: 0 563 55143 7

THE NATION'S FAVOURITE SHAKESPEARE
ISBN: 0 563 55142 9

Audio cassettes to accompany the books in this series, produced by
BBC Radio Collection:

THE NATION'S FAVOURITE POEMS
ISBN: 0 563 38987 7

THE NATION'S FAVOURITE LOVE POEMS
ISBN: 0 563 38279 1

THE NATION'S FAVOURITE COMIC POEMS
ISBN: 0 563 55850 4

THE NATION'S FAVOURITE SHAKESPEARE
ISBN: 0 563 55331 6

THE NATION'S FAVOURITE LAKELAND POEMS
ISBN: 0 563 55293 X

Available from March 2000:

THE NATION'S FAVOURITE POEMS OF CHILDHOOD
ISBN: 0 563 47727 X

The above titles are also available on CD.